THE Sun King

Rupert Murdoch in his own words

EDITED BY GEORGE BEAHM

hardie grant books
MELBOURNE · LONDON

Published in 2012 by Hardie Grant Books

Hardie Grant Books (Australia)
Ground Floor, Building 1
658 Church Street
Richmond, Victoria 3121
www.hardiegrant.com.au

Hardie Grant Books (UK)
Dudley House, North Suite
34–35 Southampton Street
London WC2E 7HF
www.hardiegrant.co.uk

Cataloguing-in-Publication data is available
from the the British Library
The Sun King: Rupert Murdoch in his own words.
ISBN 9781742704425

Cover design by Peter Daniel
Cover image courtesy of newspix.com.au
Text design by Peter Daniel
Typeset in New Baskerville
Printed and bound in the UK by CPI Group (UK) Ltd, Croydon, CR0
4YY

When you work for Rupert Murdoch you do not work for a company chairman or chief executive: you work for a Sun King. You are not a director or a manager or an editor: you are a courtier at the court of the Sun King – rewarded with money and status by a grateful king as long as you serve his purpose, dismissed outright or demoted to a remote corner of the empire when you have ceased to please him or outlived your usefulness.

All life revolves around the Sun King; all authority comes from him. He is the only one to whom allegiance must be owed, and he expects his work to be final. There are no other references but him. He is the only benchmark, and anybody of importance reports directly to him ...

The Sun King is all that matters.

— *Full Disclosure*, 1996.

Contents

Rarely Glimpsed:
Murdoch's Private Life

On being ostracised at Geelong Grammar.

I felt a loner at school, probably because of my father's position. Bullied a lot ... It made me realise that if you're going to do your job as a publisher or a principal in the media, you've got to be your own person and not have close friendships which can compromise you. That philosophy just evolved, I think.

— *Murdoch: The making of a media empire*, 1997.

On his father.

I was twenty-one when he died, so I never had the opportunity to work alongside him, which was a very hard thing. But I saw him work. In my early teenage years, I would go in on Saturday morning and watch him. In Melbourne, the big Saturday-night papers were a big deal. It just never occurred to me to do anything else.

— *Esquire* ONLINE, 11 SEPTEMBER 2008.

I just want to say that I was brought up by a father who was not rich, but who was a great journalist, and, just before he died, he bought a small paper, specifically in his will saying that he was giving me the chance to do good. I remember what he did and what he was most proud of, and for which he was hated in this country by many people for many, many years, was exposing the scandal at Gallipoli, which I remain very, very proud of.

— Uncorrected transcript of oral evidence given before the Culture, Media and Sport Select Committee, 19 July 2011.

On being a polarising public figure.

I can go into restaurants and a whole table will get up and clap if they recognise me, because they love Fox News. Other places – or even the same place – people will turn the other way. But that's okay. Look, if you run a media company, you hand out criticism. You disclose things that people don't want disclosed, because you think it's in the public interest. You're disliked for that. You get criticised and you just gotta learn to take it. You just gotta shrug it off.

— *Esquire* online, 11 September 2008.

ON IMMORTALITY.

I JUST WANT TO LIVE FOREVER. I ENJOY MYSELF TOO MUCH.

— MEDIA SUMMIT, 8 FEBRUARY 2007.

ON BEING A NORMAL PERSON.

People demonise me and think I'm more important than I am. You know, I am a fairly normal person. I don't lead a wild life or anything. My excitement is day-to-day work.

— *ESQUIRE* ONLINE, 11 SEPTEMBER 2008.

ON HIS TECH SHORTCOMINGS.

I wish I was a scientist or a physicist. There's so much to know. The biggest challenge is getting an education on all this stuff.

— *CLASH OF THE TITANS*, 2003.

ON CONSTANTLY MOVING FORWARD.

So long as I can stay mentally alert – inquiring, curious – I want to keep going. I love my wife and my children, but I don't want to sit around at home with them. We go on safaris and things like that. I can do that for a couple of weeks a year. I'm just not ready to stop, to die. Somebody talked me into writing an autobiography about six or seven years ago. And I said I'd try. We talked into a tape recorder, and after a couple of months, I said to hell with it. I was so depressed. It was like saying, 'This is the end.' I was more interested in what the hell was coming the next day or the next week.

— *ESQUIRE* ONLINE, 11 SEPTEMBER 2008.

ON HIS LEGACY.

I'm not really worried about the history books. Let the chips fall where they will. If they go back and read everything that's been written about me and use tall stories as source material, I'll be seen as a pretty terrible person. But I think that you just want to die with a good conscience and the feeling that you've been a force for good as you see it ... I'd like to feel I made a difference.

— *VANITY FAIR*, OCTOBER 1999.

ON WORKING WITH HIS CHILDREN.

What I'm proudest of is that I always had a very, very strong work ethic, and I think my children have that, too. Having my children work with me has been the greatest pleasure of my life. It's wonderful. Provided they'll listen to you once in a while.

— *ESQUIRE* ONLINE, 11 SEPTEMBER 2008.

ON HIS SONS.

When I look back on it, I wish I had more quality time with my children. I remember once taking the two boys on a three- or four-day hike around Aspen Mountain. I remember every minute of it, and they remember every minute of it. I should have done more of that sort of thing.

— *ESQUIRE* ONLINE, 11 SEPTEMBER 2008.

ON NEPOTISM.

Let me just go back over this. When the job became available of head of BSkyB, several people applied, including my son. He passed through all sorts of not just board committees but outside experts, etc., who made the conclusion that he was the right person. The press all had a field day. When he left ... [because] ... I promoted him to take charge of much wider responsibilities, we had calls from all the big shareholders, or many big shareholders, saying that it was a terrible thing to take him away because he had done such a great job.

— Uncorrected transcript of oral evidence given before the Culture, Media and Sport Select Committee, 19 July 2011.

ON HIS DAUGHTER ELISABETH'S EDUCATION.

His reaction when Elisabeth told him that she was accepted to Stanford Business School, which she planned on attending: Are you fucking crazy? No, you are not. I can give you a much better MBA of life than anybody at Stanford can give you, you know. Come work for me.

— Vanity Fair, December 2008.

ON AUSTRALIA AS HIS HOME BASE.

I think it is a lottery whatever happens to your children, but quite a compelling reason is not to have my children educated in the public-school system in England because I feel they could never get the old school tie off their necks. If [my children] want to lead a life in newspapers, if they choose that, they will grow up with better values in Australia than anywhere else I can think of.

— *Murdoch: The making of a media empire*, 1997.

ON THE BREAKDOWN OF HIS SECOND MARRIAGE.

I don't want to go into it, but it happened over a period. It was progressive ... There are never any blacks or whites in these situations. It's always mixtures of grey. You always feel very sad about these things, but you've got to get on with life. You go through a pretty bad period of mixed emotions and self-doubt, but there it is.

— *Vanity Fair*, October 1999.

ON HIS WANDERING HEART.

In response to his mother who, after the dissolution of his second marriage, warned him that 'you're going to be very, very lonely and the first desiring female who comes along will snap you up.': Don't be ridiculous, Mum, I'm far too old for that.

— *VANITY FAIR*, OCTOBER 2008.

ON WENDI DENG.

To Gary Davey (News Corp.'s Star TV CEO), who introduced him to Wendi Deng, the junior staffer who became Murdoch's third wife: You're probably wondering why Wendi isn't back from holiday. Well, she's with me, and chances are she won't be coming back to Star TV.

— *VANITY FAIR*, DECEMBER 2008.

In a conversation with his children: I just wanted to tell you – hmmm ... humm ... ahhh – I've met a nice Chinese lady.

— *VANITY FAIR*, DECEMBER 2008.

Oh, yes, she's very tough. Successful men need a critical wife; it brings him down to earth.

— NEWSER.COM, 22 JULY 2011.

Political Movers, Shakers
and Moneymakers

On President George Bush and the Iraq War.

We can't back down now. I think Bush is acting very morally, very correctly, and I think he is going to go on with it. The fact is, a lot of the world can't accept the idea that America is the one superpower in the world.

He will either go down in history as a very great president or he'll crash and burn. I'm optimistic it will be the former by a ratio of two to one. Bush has surprised everyone. Even his opponents have a great deal more respect for him than they did when he was elected. One senses he is a man of great character and deep humility.

— *The Guardian* online, 11 February 2003.

On Barack Obama.

On the then-senator's campaign for presidency: He is a rock star. It's fantastic. I love what he is saying about education ... I am anxious to meet him. I want to see if he will walk the walk.

— huffingtonpost.com, 29 May 2008.

Obama's trouble is he thinks he can make a great speech – he's a great speaker – and it will be done. But nothing gets done.

He doesn't listen to anybody. The other day he invited [New York City] Mayor Bloomberg to a day of golf at Martha's Vineyard. Bloomberg said it was a pleasant day. In conversation he [gave Obama] a few ideas … He said it was like verbal ping pong. He came back and said, 'I never met in my life such an arrogant man.'

— *FINANCIAL REVIEW* ONLINE, 5 NOVEMBER 2010.

On Obama's plan for bigger government: I think Barack Obama would describe himself as a pragmatic leftist but he's not an extremist. I think he sees himself as a president for change, and that involves bigger government. He's made no secret of that. I think that's dangerous.

— HUFFINGTONPOST.COM, 7 JULY 2009.

So Obama has thrown in his lot with Silicon Valley paymasters who threaten all software creators with piracy, plain thievery.

— TWITTER, 15 JANUARY 2012.

ON THEN-SENATOR HILLARY CLINTON AS A PRESIDENTIAL CANDIDATE.

I would just say that she's a very considerable, very intelligent lady, very calculating. I think that unfortunately she's a bit divisive. People think, 'Oh, God, another eight years of Clintons.' She's way to the left ... which is okay. But I'm not really frightened of her in terms of foreign policy and social things, and defence. If anything, she might overcompensate for image there. She would certainly be a lot stronger, and subtler, and better than her husband was. (Laughter) I'm not talking about foreign policy. Defence.

— MEDIA SUMMIT, 8 FEBRUARY 2007.

ON FORMER HOUSE SPEAKER NEWT GINGRICH AS A PRESIDENTIAL CANDIDATE.

The man I would like to see get into it ... I don't know about winning it, but I'd love to see him, because he lifted the whole debate incredibly, would be Newt Gingrich. I think he's the most brilliant and interesting person out there at the moment. Doesn't say be the best president, I just think he would make all the primaries very, very interesting, and a lot more serious.

— MEDIA SUMMIT, 8 FEBRUARY 2007.

ON NEW YORK MAYOR MICHAEL BLOOMBERG AS PRESIDENT.

But he can run a clean government, efficient government ... And he would be an extremely interesting candidate, and a very able chief executive. You wouldn't get an abler chief executive for the country ... I just think he's done a superb job in New York, and, you know, he's a very genuine public servant. He's made a lot of money, huge, more than anyone realises, and he's all about giving it back now. He's a very admirable person.

— MEDIA SUMMIT, 8 FEBRUARY 2007.

ON ARIZONA SENATOR JOHN MCCAIN'S RUN FOR PRESIDENCY.

McCain is a friend of mine. He's a patriot. But he's unpredictable. Doesn't seem to know much about the economy. He has been in Congress a long time, and you have to make a lot of compromises. So what's he really stand for? ... I think he has a lot of problems.

— HUFFINGTONPOST.COM, 29 MAY 2008.

ON CNN COMMENTATOR GLENN BECK.

There's a guy on Fox who started on CNN called Glenn Beck. He is a little bit of an actor; he looks in the camera all the time. He's very genuine, extremely well read, libertarian, doesn't make any secret of it. He says don't trust the government, don't trust me, just trust yourselves. He's hit a nerve. Millions – millions – watch him at five in the afternoon!

— *FINANCIAL REVIEW* ONLINE, 5 NOVEMBER 2010.

ON CONSERVATIVE FOX NEWS ANCHOR BILL O'REILLY.

Bill O'Reilly gets Hillary Clinton on. He's disgraceful the way he gives her such an easy ride. We're beating the shit out of CNN.

— *FINANCIAL REVIEW* ONLINE, 5 NOVEMBER 2010.

On the well-regarded official Steve Jobs
biography by Walter Isaacson.

Interesting but unfair, family must hate.

— Twitter, 3 January 2012.

ON MEDIA MOGUL TED TURNER.

We were good friends. I stayed on his ranch, we used to chat for stories and everything else. Then he came out about a week after I said I was going to start a news channel, which was only a throwaway remark at a chamber of commerce luncheon in Boston. And he made such a fuss about it. We never said we'd get on with it. We said we'd look at it, we cared to do it, but we didn't actually put a time on it. And I said to mutual friends, it's play-acting, we're really good friends. And they said no no no, you don't understand, he really does hate you.

— *THE MURDOCH MISSION: THE DIGITAL TRANSFORMATION OF A MEDIA EMPIRE*, 2002.

ON CAMILLAGATE.

In a public statement issued by RM's spokesperson on the scandal sparked by the publication of a transcript of an illegally recorded conversation between Prince Charles and his then-married mistress (now wife), Camilla Parker Bowles, in New Idea: [He had] no knowledge of negotiations to buy the tape, nor that *New Idea* had it or had published it. He wished he had ... Any suggestion of 'collusion or conspiracy' between companies in which he has an interest is totally without foundation.

— *SYDNEY MORNING HERALD*, 31 JULY 2011.

ON FORMER PRIME MINISTER
MARGARET THATCHER.

So I ask you to join me in a toast: To a woman whose name has become a synonym for liberty and strength ... Margaret Thatcher ... This evening, I speak as more than an admirer of Margaret Thatcher. I speak as a person grateful for the opportunities this nation has given me – and the opportunities she has created for every other individual in Great Britain ... Over the years, the word 'Thatcherite' has been tossed around carelessly. Sometimes it is even used as an epithet. For all of us here, however, the word 'Thatcherite' is a source of inspiration.

— *THE GUARDIAN*, 21 OCTOBER 2010.

....

On her refusal to back President Reagan in his 1983 invasion of Grenada: She's gone out of her mind. I don't know what she's about. I just think she's very overtired. I know it sounds silly but I think it is a very human thing ... She's run out of puff. She's not listening to any of her friends.

— *ARROGANT AUSSIE: THE RUPERT MURDOCH STORY*, 1985.

ON FORMER PRIME MINISTER TONY BLAIR.

Last year we helped the Labor government in Canberra. I could even imagine supporting Tony Blair.

— *THE INDEPENDENT*, 11 FEBRUARY 1998.

....

If the British press is to be believed, today is all part of a Blair–Murdoch flirtation. If that flirtation is ever consummated, Tony, I suspect we will end up making love like two porcupines – very carefully.

— *THE INDEPENDENT*, 11 FEBRUARY 1998.

....

RM's characterisation of Tony Blair: ... [He has a] puppy-dog, youthful, company-lawyer image.

— *THE INDEPENDENT*, 11 FEBRUARY 1998.

....

On Tony Blair and the BBC: Tony Blair – perhaps I shouldn't repeat this conversation – told me yesterday that he was in Delhi last week. And he turned on the BBC world service to see what was happening in New Orleans [in the wake of Hurricane Katrina]. And he said it was just full of hate of America and gloating about our troubles. And that was his government. Well, his government-owned thing [the BBC].

— *USA TODAY*, 17 SEPTEMBER 2005.

On Judith Regan.

On the controversial book editor/publisher's tabloid sensibilities, which made her a rising star in the book industry by championing controversial books, among them OJ Simpson's book, If I Did It, *which was subsequently killed*: Judith was very good at Simon & Schuster, where we noted that she had a great sort of popular feel for what could sell, and did some very good best-sellers for us to start with. But then it was sort of downhill ... she just was not a team player. That's putting it mildly ... She did have ability. She wasn't for us.

— MEDIA SUMMIT, 8 FEBRUARY 2007.

ON ITALIAN PRIME MINISTER SILVIO BERLUSCONI.

Embroiled in a sex scandal involving a 17-year-old girl known as 'Ruby the Heart Stealer', the randy PM asserted that Murdoch used his media assets to trash-talk him: It's nonsense. There was a lot of comment a few months ago when he lowered taxes everywhere in Italy, all business taxes, except on satellite television which he doubled. And he does own the competition, and that tax did not apply when he owned [the competition]. That was business. Now we've not retaliated or said anything about that at all. I don't control what the editor of the *Times* of London says or the *Economist* says attacking him. *The New York Times*, God knows I have no influence there.

— HUFFINGTONPOST.COM, 29 MAY 2008.

ON ROBERT MAXWELL.

Yesterday Mr Maxwell called me a moth-eaten kangaroo. I'd like to point out that I haven't yet got to that stage.

— BBC NEWS ONLINE, 30 JANUARY 2011.

ON TIBET.

Defending China's policies in Tibet, where Buddhist monks self-immolate in record numbers protesting China's involvement: I have heard cynics who say [the Dalai Lama is] a very political old monk shuffling around in Gucci shoes ... It was a pretty terrible old autocratic society out of the Middle Ages. Maybe I'm falling for their propaganda, but it was an authoritarian, medieval society without any basic services ... The problem they have is that half the people of Tibet still think that the Dalai Lama is the son of God.

— *VANITY FAIR*, OCTOBER 1999.

A Media Empire

ON PRINTER'S INK IN HIS BLOOD.

My whole life has been with newspapers and so has my father's. You could say my destiny is to be in love with newspapers.

— *ARROGANT AUSSIE: THE RUPERT MURDOCH STORY*, 1985.

ON TABLOIDS.

They're different animals. You've got to make people want to read 'em. They've got to have some fun and a bit of edge. Agendas up to a point, and certainly crusades. But I don't call all those shots. I haven't got the time.

— *TIME*, 28 JUNE 2007.

On the *Adelaide News*'s libel charge.

In a 1959 editorial, written by RM, on the Adelaide News'*s headlines about the murder of a young girl; the rabble-rousing coverage resulted in Murdoch's company being charged with 'nine counts of libel, including three of seditious libel'*: The *News* has AT NO TIME alleged any crime by any member of the government, the Supreme Court, or even the South Australian Police. However, we conceive it as our duty to report all statements in such an important matter ... We never claimed that [the accused] is innocent – merely that he must be shown to be guilty beyond all doubt before being hanged. The *News* sees it as its duty to fight always not only for justice to be done but for justice to appear to be done. WE MAINTAIN THIS STAND AND WILL CONTINUE, WITH PRIDE, TO FIGHT FOR THIS IDEA.

— *Arrogant Aussie: The Rupert Murdoch story*, 1985.

ON MOST NEWSPAPERS' FAILURE TO KEEP UP WITH
DIGITAL TECHNOLOGIES.

Most newspaper companies still have their heads in the sand, but other media companies are aggressive.

— THEDAILYBEAST.COM, 12 FEBRUARY 2006.

ON THE CHALLENGES OF WORKING WITH
NEWSPAPER EDITORS.

Just because I haven't managed to get the right working relationship with every single editor I've appointed doesn't for a minute suggest that I'm ruthless. In fact if you'd known the precise reasoning at the time ... and the sort of settlement these people got. I think one would consider me – a lot of people did consider me – rather ridiculously soft ... I'm far too easy-going as a rule.

— *ARROGANT AUSSIE: THE RUPERT MURDOCH STORY*, 1985.

ON THE FUTURE OF PRINT NEWSPAPERS.

I just love communicating with people; newspapers are the way of doing it. I don't care what platform our news appears on. Across the country today, some people share that view, and others are just frightened. All of them are going to have a hard time. [The] [a]verage newspaper [is] down 10 to 30 per cent in total ad revenue, and that means their profit margins. They have made every economy possible in production, but not in journalism. They are going to do that. It gives a huge opportunity for *The Wall Street Journal*. A paper's servicing the 10 per cent of the most influential, most educated people in a community is a huge opportunity. I think print will be there. We have a big, wide free site, but when you get into what we have today, with a lot of analysis and detail, people will pay for that.

— *Barron's* ONLINE, 28 MAY 2008.

On the power of newspapers.

A newspaper can create great controversies, stir up arguments within the community, can throw lights on injustices, just as it can do the opposite: hide things, be a great power for evil.

— theworld.org, 14 July 2011.

On newspapers taking on debt.

There have been a lot of newspaper deals done in the last ten years in which people have taken on ridiculous debt. If you look at the Tribune Company, their big papers – the *LA Times*, *Chicago Tribune* – I bet you they're still making money individually. But they can't pay their interest bills. Bankruptcy doesn't mean the end of a newspaper. It just means that someone's going to buy them from a bank.

— PAIDCONTENT.ORG, 28 MAY 2009.

On suffering cash flow problems.

The Pittsburgh National Bank demanded $10 million at a time when the News *was unable to service the debt*: It was horrific. *Horrific!* The chief loan officer said, 'Liquidate your company.' All for ten million dollars!

— MURDOCH: THE MAKING OF A MEDIA EMPIRE, 1997.

After the bank crisis was resolved in the News's favour.

Chief credit officers of small banks who were two- to three-million-dollar participants had no qualms about telling us to liquidate the whole twenty billion dollars of assets. In fact, one or two seemed to enjoy it.

— *Murdoch: The making of a media empire*, 1997.

On buying Dow Jones, which owns The Wall Street Journal.

We're cooling on the idea of buying Dow Jones. *The Wall Street Journal* is obviously a wonderful brand. But I don't think we'd ever get it or they'd ever sell it.

— Media Summit, 8 February 2007.

On negotiations to buy The Wall Street Journal.

A year ago they made $81 million after tax and paid $80 million in dividends, and you can't grow a company that way.

— *The New York Times*, 4 May 2007.

ON ACQUIRING *THE WALL STREET JOURNAL.*

If anything you will find us trying to set a higher bar. So we want to see a better paper. It's already a great paper but everything can always improve. And we'll be there encouraging you and helping you in every way we can.

Our aim is pretty simple. We have to entertain, inform, enrich all our readers in their lives and in their businesses. We must be the pre-eminent source of financial information and comment in the world. And we must put ourselves beyond there being any doubt in that regard.

— *WAR AT* THE WALL STREET JOURNAL: *INSIDE THE STRUGGLE TO CONTROL AN AMERICAN BUSINESS EMPIRE,* 2010.

ON THE HIDDEN COST OF *THE WALL STREET JOURNAL.*

The price of the *Journal* is $60 plus vitriol.

— *TIME,* 28 JUNE 2007.

On having bought *The Wall Street Journal*.

It's bullshit to say we're going to dumb down *The Wall Street Journal*. We didn't dumb down the London *Times* – we made the London *Times*. *The Sunday Times*, too. Are they a little more popular than they were? Yes. They are populist papers. You've got to listen to readers.

— *Esquire* online, 11 September 2008.

On the aftermath of News Corp.'s acquisition of Dow Jones.

I am deeply gratified at the level of support we have received from the Bancroft family and its trustees. Given the Bancrofts' long and distinguished history as custodian of Dow Jones, we appreciate how difficult this decision was for some family members. I want to offer the Bancrofts my thanks, and an assurance that our company and my family will be equally strong custodians.

— News Corp. press release, 1 August 2007.

AND WHEN THE HONEYMOON WAS OVER ...

They're taking five billion dollars out of me and want to keep control in an industry in crisis! They can't sell their company and still control it – that's not how it works. I'm sorry!

— *TIME*, 28 JUNE 2007.

ON CRITICISMS THAT *WALL STREET JOURNAL* READERS' OPINION OF THE PAPER DIMINISHED BECAUSE OF NEWS CORP.'S IMPENDING OWNERSHIP.

We're going to build a fucking great paper and I do not give a fuck what New York or the media has to say about it! We'll build the world's best paper!

— *WAR AT* THE WALL STREET JOURNAL: *INSIDE THE STRUGGLE TO CONTROL AN AMERICAN BUSINESS EMPIRE*, 2010.

On Fox News being fair and balanced.

The real story about Fox is the business story. The real thing is by being fair and balanced by putting on both sides all the time we really have changed the political equation in this country. People think we're conservative but we're not conservative ... Bill O'Reilly is not a newscaster; he's a commentator, but he's on both sides ... Brit Hume is not a politician.

— *Financial Times* online, 6 October 2006.

On Fox's competition.

Our company has a history of challenging the established – and often stagnant – media with new products and services for television viewers around the world. Perhaps our first and best-known effort to offer new choices to consumers in the broadcasting arena came with the establishment of the Fox network in 1986. Fox brought much-needed competition to the 'Big 3' broadcast networks at a time when conventional wisdom said it couldn't be done.

— Testimony given to the US House Committee on the Judiciary, 8 May 2003.

On Fox Interactive Media (FIM).

We're launching this new unit after months of internal study and discussion among News Corp. senior management from all key divisions. Across the board, we believe no other media company has been as successful at creating distinctive content and finding ways to distribute it over every conceivable platform to mass audiences around the world. We're confident this success will translate to the Internet. We believe the time is right for the launch of FIM and we're committed to devoting the resources to make it one of the premier companies on the Web.

— News Corp. public announcement, 15 July 2005.

ON PRESENTING NEWS AND ENTERTAINMENT.

A really integrated media company has to be in the production of entertainment. It also has to be in news reporting. For both, the question is one of how do you present it? In magazine form or television form? For all those things, you've got to have a foot in the creative processes. Making movies is part of that. I went to entertainment not to get into entertainment. It was part of a broad strategy to get into the media industry, the heart of the media industry. I know you can't really talk about one global economy, but there really is. There are certain things that are common. Hollywood is still the magnet for the most talent. Studios here still have the pre-eminent position. So if one owns a studio, it's a great opportunity.

— *MURDOCH: THE MAKING OF A MEDIA EMPIRE*, 1997.

ON THE THEN-STRUGGLING LONDON NEWSPAPER, *THE TIMES*, WHICH HE BOUGHT IN 1981.

To buy *The Times* would be a highly irresponsible thing to do for your shareholders.

— *ARROGANT AUSSIE: THE RUPERT MURDOCH STORY*, 1985.

IN RESPONSE TO *THE TIMES* STAFFERS WHO WERE SCEPTICAL OF HIS CLAIMS THAT HE'D GUARANTEE EDITORIAL INDEPENDENCE.

I can sell myself to you as the least of the alternative evils. As regard the guarantees themselves ... I think I have locked myself in, particularly with the power I have given [to the national directors] of absolute right of hiring and firing of editors and given them the right to be a self-perpetuating body ... What if I found a way of tearing up all those guarantees and fired an editor? The answer is there would be a terrible public stink and it would destroy the paper ... I get on with these people or I get out. Otherwise I would destroy what I am attempting to buy.

— *ARROGANT AUSSIE: THE RUPERT MURDOCH STORY*, 1985.

TO A *SUNDAY TIMES* EXECUTIVE AT WAPPING.

You fuckwit! You bastard! Get this fucking newspaper out!

— *RUPERT MURDOCH: THE UNTOLD STORY OF THE WORLD'S GREATEST MEDIA WIZARD*, 2011.

ON NEWSPAPERS' ELITISM.

Most of the media are local monopolies. They've got elitist journalists coming out of journalism school and they look down on their audiences. They are not in touch at all with the average middle class guy with the fifty thousand, sixty thousand dollar job living out in the suburbs living a normal life. Look at what's happening in Long Island [New York]. The taxes have gone up so much that there is a major flight to the south. Do you get reports about it in the Long Island *Newsday* – no. The reason for these taxes, I don't know, but there is a major flight away from high taxes, big pieces of their discretionary income are going on this, and much against their will. Second and third generation people are moving to the south or the west – not the far west because they would get hit again in California.

— *FINANCIAL TIMES* ONLINE, 6 OCTOBER 2006.

On American journalism.

The problem with American journalism is that they simply don't know how to compete. They all go to journalism school and listen to failed editors dressed up as professors.

— *The Age*, November 1983.

On his patented brand of tabloid journalism.

In light of his purchasing The Boston Globe *in 1982, which he subsequently sold for US$1.1 billion*: Now I don't think that's to say *The Boston Globe* will become a worse paper. It may become a better paper because of us. All I'm saying is I think it's unnatural for a good tabloid *not* to outsell a good broadsheet ... Tabloid journalism has gone out of fashion in America, but I think it will come back. There's a market out there for papers that are not ashamed to include some human interest, that are not ashamed to entertain people ... There's a tendency today to judge tabloids by more traditional standards of journalism.

There's an elitist attitude out there. One problem is that journalism students today are taught that papers like *The New York Times* and *The Washington Post* are the models, that what those papers do is responsible and what someone else does is irresponsible. By the time these kids are on the street [looking for work], they have a cynical approach to anything that is not traditional. Their goal seems to be to have Robert Redford play them in a movie.

— *Boston*, May 1983.

ON HIS ACQUISITION OF CHICAGO'S *SUN-TIMES*.

Basically, we neither plan or intend any substantial changes in the newspaper and we would strive to maintain the newspaper's high standards and its reputation in the community ... It will not look like any of our other papers so much as it will look like the *Sun-Times* in today's form ... I will be approaching the task of continuing the *Sun-Times* with great seriousness and no little humility. I plan to spend a great deal of time in Chicago in the early stages of our ownership.

— PRESS CONFERENCE, 1 NOVEMBER 1983.

ON WHY READERS SHOULD PASS OVER THE SUNDAY EDITION OF *THE NEW YORK TIMES*.

Some of them you get tired of reading. *The New York Times* on Sunday is very much the worst issue they put out for the week ... Not much gets printed on Sunday. The fact is they write for Monday, Tuesday, Wednesday, Thursday. Come Friday all those people are out at the Hamptons – their best reporters and editors. And it's leftovers on Sunday. They don't have their best people on.

— *THE MURDOCH MISSION: THE DIGITAL TRANSFORMATION OF A MEDIA EMPIRE*, 2002.

A *Post* HEADLINE.

Ted Turner: Is He Nuts?

— *The New Yorker* ONLINE, 2 JULY 2007.

A *Boston Herald* HEADLINE ON EDWARD KENNEDY.

Fat Boy.

— *The New Yorker* ONLINE, 2 JULY 2007.

ON THE *New York Post*.

We're very proud of what we do at all our papers. And we just feel insulted by the coverage. We've got more than 50,000 people [in News Corp.]. We make mistakes here and there. But there's nothing wrong with the *Post* – most people would prefer to read it before they go to the *Times*. There's such a thing as a popular newspaper and an unpopular elite newspaper. They play different roles. We have both kinds. Just like we have the Fox network with *American Idol* and *24*, and we also have the National Geographic Channel. It's hard for outsiders to understand that.

— *Time*, 28 JUNE 2007.

ON GOOGLE PAYING FOR CONTENT TAKEN FROM THE PRINT MEDIA.

I don't know if they can afford to do that. If they were to pay everybody for everything they took, from every newspaper in the world and every magazine, they wouldn't have any profits left.

They have devised a brilliant search engine that scrapes all the material published in the world and on the back of that they sell search, but they don't pay for the raw material. We have to do something about that.

The news industry spends a fortune in collecting its news … and it needs to be paid for it, and there's not enough advertising to go around.

— WALLSTREETPIT.COM, 19 NOVEMBER 2009.

ON NEWSPAPERS V. BLOGGERS.

In conversation with Walt Mossberg, who asked about the iPad and content, Apple's Steve Jobs replied: I don't want to see us descend into a nation of bloggers ... I think we need editorial oversight now more than ever. Anything we can do to help newspapers find new ways of expression that will help them get paid, I am all for.

— MEDIAITE.COM, 2 JUNE 2010.

Murdoch's response: From the point of view of our democracy, it's very important to have good, edited newspapers, responsible information disseminated, and views, everywhere. And if we just descend to blogs, which a lot of people can't distinguish between the good and the bad – and most of them are bad and crazy ... [Steve Jobs] was saying this is really important.

— MEDIAITE.COM, 2 JUNE 2010.

ON CARVING OUT A NICHE IN MEDIA.

Content is king, but you've still got to get distribution. If you have the leverage of a major distributor, you've still got a long way to go developing content, but it gives you a certain security – and it means if you're really producing great content, you've got no excuse for it not getting to the proper audience ... You can do it, but not if you're just doing the same thing as somebody else, someone that's entrenched. [You have to] get into it in a different way: You've got to look for a gap, where competitors in a market have grown lazy [and] lost contact with the readers or the viewers. Viewers are a bit different: the network concept is going fast.

— WEBPUBLISHINGBLOG.COM, 15 NOVEMBER 2005.

ON THE BBC.

Much of what passes for quality on British television is no more than a reflection of the narrow elite which controls it and has always thought that its tastes were synonymous with quality.

— BBC NEWS ONLINE, 1 AUGUST 2007.

ON NEWS CORP. V. STATE-SUPPORTED BROADCASTING.

We are about change and progress, not about protectionism through legislation and cronyism. We are about vigorous competition, not about whingeing or distorting the market. We are about daring and doing for ourselves, not about riding on someone else's coat tails.

— *THE MURDOCH ARCHIPELAGO*, 2003.

ON HIS ACQUISITION OF *THE SUN*.

The most important thing to remember is that the new *Sun* will still be a paper that CARES ... The new *Sun* will have a conscience. It will never forget its radical traditions. It will be truly independent, but politically mightily aware ... It will never, ever sit on fences. It will never, ever be boring.

— *MURDOCH: THE MAKING OF A MEDIA EMPIRE*, 1997.

ON THE POPULAR 'PAGE THREE GIRLS' IN *THE SUN*.

The feminists get pissed off, but they've even quieted down now. They're so harmless, those pictures. They really are. There's nothing pornographic. Bare top. That's all it is ...

— *THE MURDOCH MISSION: THE DIGITAL TRANSFORMATION OF A MEDIA EMPIRE,* 2002.

ON A NEWSPAPER'S POSITION, TO HAROLD EVANS, *THE SUNDAY TIMES* EDITOR.

My chief area of concern about the paper is one I have raised with you several times: the paper's stand on major issues. Of course it takes attitudes, but I fail to find any consistency in them, anything that indicates unmistakeably the clear position of conscience that a great newspaper must be seen to hold. Just what that position is, it is your duty to define, and it cannot be mine. But it must be defined with clarity and authority and even repetition.

— *MURDOCH: THE MAKING OF A MEDIA EMPIRE,* 1997.

On accusations that NDS (News Corp.'s pay-TV smartcard security unit) is promoting piracy attacks on the competition.

Seems every competitor and enemy piling on with lies and libels. So bad, easy to hit back hard, which preparing ... Enemies many different agendas, but worst old toffs and right wingers who still want last century's status quo with their monopolies ... Let's have it on! Choice, freedom of thought and markets, individual personal responsibility.

—Twitter, 29 March 2012.

On News Corp.'s broadband penetration.

News Corp. will work aggressively to ... make broadband available throughout the United States, particularly in rural areas. Broadband solutions for all Americans could come from partnering with other satellite broadband providers, DSL providers, or new potential broadband providers using broadband over power line systems, or from other emerging technologies. News Corp. believes it is critical that consumers have choices that compete with cable's video and broadband services on capability, quality and price.

— Testimony given to the US House Committee on the Judiciary, 8 May 2003.

On CNN's faults.

We are a news organisation. To be a meaningful broadcaster you have to have news. We will do one [news channel], and it will be much better than CNN. I watch it when I get on my exercise machine in the morning. There are long commercial breaks and it's quite repetitive.

— *Murdoch: The making of a media empire*, 1997.

On book publishing.

Look, we reject books all the time, publish too many, not politically, don't get me wrong. Everyone's publishing too many books to get any space in [major US book chain] Barnes & Noble or anywhere.

— *The Wall Street Journal* online, 6 June 2007.

Musings of a
Machiavellian Media Mogul

ON RISKING THE JOBS OF 200 EMPLOYEES WHO WORKED AT *NEWS OF THE WORLD*.

When a company closes down, it is natural for people to lose their jobs. We have in this case made – and I am making this continually – every effort to see that those people are employed in other divisions of the company, if they are not part of the small group ... involved with criminality.

— UNCORRECTED TRANSCRIPT OF ORAL EVIDENCE GIVEN BEFORE THE CULTURE, MEDIA AND SPORT SELECT COMMITTEE, 19 JULY 2011.

ON CRITICS AND ENEMIES.

I'm not looking for a legacy, and you'll never shut up the critics. I've been around fifty years. When you're a catalyst for change, you make enemies – and I'm proud of the ones I've got.

— *TIME*, 28 JUNE 2007.

ON SUCCESS AND SCAR TISSUE.

I'm a catalyst for change. You can't be an outsider and be successful over thirty years without leaving a certain amount of scar tissue around the place.

— BBC NEWS ONLINE, 1 AUGUST 2007.

On the printers' union strike after Murdoch moved the London *Times* to Wapping.

We had a horrible strike … They all came out on a Saturday night and a Wednesday night. It was like a big night out for them. And the police would be there, and the horses. And they'd be throwing darts into the back of the horses, who would rear up. And the television lights would come on. And we – what was really interesting was the major industrial figures. People like the head of ICI and so on went on the BBC and said, 'This is not the British way to conduct relations.' But we couldn't get to first base. Anyway, after a couple of weeks I had a deal with … the head of the union, secretly … And I never heard from her again. She couldn't sell it to the union at all.

So they stayed out. And a year later they settled that they'd never come back and take one week pay for every year they'd been working for me. And, which was half of what I offered a year before. And that was it.

That was an epic battle. It was the first major – in fifty years or certainly, forty years – industrial dispute that had been won in Britain by … a private employer.

— *Uncommon Knowledge*, 5 February 2010.

ON THE ECONOMY.

The average family is squeezed to death, living hand to mouth. For the most part, the country is suffering terribly, and people are cutting back. The next thing you'll see is some unemployment. Starting to see it in England. Most of Europe is negative or flat. Australia is still booming because it is like one big quarry for China and India.

There's a lot to put right. We're going to be dependent on oil for a long time. It will take ten to fifteen years for investment in nuclear and wind and others to take effect. We've got to do something about it right here and now. I would let people drill off the West Coast. We didn't buy Alaska to save a couple of elk. Long-term, I'm very optimistic. There are 6.5 billion people in the world; 3.5 billion engaged in the economy. There is going to be inflationary pressure; the world is getting wealthier and wealthier.

— *BARRON'S* ONLINE, 28 MAY 2008.

WHEN ASKED, 'OF ALL THE THINGS IN YOUR BUSINESS EMPIRE, WHAT GIVES YOU THE MOST PLEASURE?'

Being involved with the editor of a paper in a day-to-day campaign. Trying to influence people.

— *THE NEW YORKER* ONLINE, 2 JULY 2007.

ON HIS PRESENCE IN THE NEWSROOM.

I'd love to wander around. I'm not going to have much time to do it. I enjoy popular journalism. I must say I enjoy it more than what you would call quality journalism.

— *THE NEW YORKER* ONLINE, 2 JULY 2007.

ON ACCOUNTABILITY.

Look, when a paper starts to go bad and goes down the drain, the buck stops with me. Shareholders don't ring the editor, they ring me. And that once or twice has led to very unhappy but necessary decisions. I made mistakes but had to change them. It's been very seldom.

— *THE WALL STREET JOURNAL* ONLINE, 6 JUNE 2007.

ON ACCUSATIONS OF *NEWS OF THE WORLD* BREAKING THE LAW TO GET NEWS SCOOPS.

No, I think that's totally wrong. There is no excuse for breaking the law at any time. There is an excuse, if I may say so, and I think rightful, for all newspapers when they wish to, to campaign for a change in the law, but never to break it.

— UNCORRECTED TRANSCRIPT OF ORAL EVIDENCE GIVEN BEFORE THE CULTURE, MEDIA AND SPORT SELECT COMMITTEE, 19 JULY 2011.

AN EMPLOYEE'S RESPONSE.

In an interview by Stuart Varney of Fox Business News, RM deflects his employee's question with 'I'm not talking about that issue at all today.' Varney responds: Okay. No worries, Mr Chairman. That's fine with me.

— *THE WALL STREET JOURNAL* ONLINE, 9 JULY 2009.

ON FIGHTING BACK AS A DETERRENCE.

When someone's trying to run you down, you try to protect yourself so that, the next time, someone else doesn't try to run you down.

— *THE NEW YORK TIMES*, 6 FEBRUARY 1984.

ON *POST* WRITERS' ASSERTION THAT 'IT'S OUR NEWSPAPER, TOO' IN A PETITION.

Oh no, it's not. When you pay the losses you can say it's your paper too. It's *my* newspaper. You just work here and don't you forget it.

— *ARROGANT AUSSIE: THE RUPERT MURDOCH STORY*, 1985.

ON HIS DECISION TO FIRE 148 *POST* STAFFERS WHO HAD SIGNED THE PETITION.

The *Post* proposes, on a one-time basis, the right to terminate members of the staff, with appropriate severance pay, who in its judgement are incompatible with the new management's publishing concept.

— *ARROGANT AUSSIE: THE RUPERT MURDOCH STORY*, 1985.

On employees unhappy
working for him.

You don't like it, quit.

— *Clash of the Titans*, 2003.

ON AMERICAN UNIONS.

American unions have taught their members to expect a great
deal more than a day's pay for a great deal less than a day's work.

— *THE NEW YORK TIMES*, 21 APRIL 1978.

ON CONFLICT OF INTEREST.

I don't think that a newspaper should own outside interests ...
By owning something outside journalism you lay yourself open
for attack. And newspapers should be above that.

— *ARROGANT AUSSIE: THE RUPERT MURDOCH STORY*, 1985.

On monopolies.

Ours is a company that has prospered by injecting competition into industries and countries that for a long time favoured monopoly suppliers. Britain is a case in point. Ever since television first became available, the government has favoured BBC, allowing it to use tax revenues to finance whatever programming the elite thought appropriate to put on air.

When we launched Sky Television, we had to cut through a thicket of rules, regulations and customs that were designed to preserve the broadcast monopoly – or, by then, duopoly – that had existed for decades. Through perseverance, and at considerable expense, we have been able to do that.

— *The Murdoch Mission: The digital transformation of a media empire*, 2002.

....

Monopoly is a terrible thing – till you have it.

— *Clash of the Titans*, 2003.

ON CONSCIENCE AND NEWSPAPERS' SOCIETAL ROLE.

It is in balancing these three interests – those of our share-holders, our customers and our host governments – that our most important master comes into play: our consciences.

We have special powers: we can help to set the agenda of political discussion. We can uncover government misdeeds and bring them to light. We can decide what television fare to offer children on a rainy Saturday morning. We can affect the culture by glorifying or demonising certain behaviour, such as the use of drugs.

> — *The Murdoch Mission: The digital transformation of a media empire*, 2002.

ON THE CITIZEN'S RIGHT TO KNOW.

The basic premise of the democracy we live in must be the citizen's right to know, and if we do not publish what we know, if we know the facts that are in the public interest and are of importance and do not publish them, then we do not deserve our freedom.

> — *The Murdoch Archipelago*, 2003.

On conscience and consistency in a newspaper's editorial views.

In a letter to Harold Evans, the editor of The Sunday Times: My chief area of concern about the paper is one I have raised with you several times: the paper's stand on major issues. Of course it takes attitudes, but I fail to find any consistency in them, anything that indicates the clear position of conscience that a great newspaper must be seen to hold. Just what that position is, it is your duty to define, and it cannot be defined by me. But it must be defined with clarity and authority and even repetition.

— *The Murdoch Archipelago*, 2003.

On his deep-rooted ties to Australia.

To Bruce Gyngell, the chairman of the Australian Broadcast Tribunal in 1979: Who else has risked his every penny, his reputation and his career in fighting for what he believes is right for this country? Who else has risked everything to establish a national newspaper across the length and breadth of this nation? No nation this size or age at this stage of its development has had national media before. But Australia has. It is a time when it is searching for identity and purpose. Sooner or later we have to do some uniting in this country. I started *The Australian* fifteen years ago as a dream and nearly $30 million has gone into making that dream a reality and I certainly did not do it to come here today to be called a foreigner or to be punished for standing up to the entrenched monopolies of this country. The story of News Limited since 1954 has been fighting these other great media establishments which have gone to any lengths to try to stamp me out. You will remember a company I used to work for was rather active in that at some stage, at many stages.

— *The Murdoch Archipelago*, 2003.

ON STRIKING WHILE THE IRON IS HOT.

There is a moment in time when the opportunity presents itself to leap forward and achieve great success. There is no doubt in my mind that the moment is now for Fox. We intend to seize this moment and propel our network forward to the forefront of American broadcasting.

— *CLASH OF THE TITANS*, 2003.

ON HIMSELF.

Big media companies are always built by individuals, not committees or boards.

— *VANITY FAIR*, OCTOBER 1999.

MURDOCH'S MOTTO.

FORTUNE FAVOURS THE BRAVE.

— *CLASH OF THE TITANS*, 2003.

On News Corp.'s critics.

Our company has always been about imagining the future and then making that vision a reality.

News was once a small publisher of newspapers in one region of Australia. There have always been those who doubted us. Who doubted us when we expanded to Great Britain. When we launched a fourth broadcast network in the United States. When we launched a cable news network. When we bought MySpace.

And they have been proven wrong. At each step, we took a risk, and re-invented ourselves. The unique potential – and duty – of a media company are to help its audiences connect to the issues that define our time.

We are only at the beginning of this mission, and we have a long way to go.

— Speech for News Corp. employees, 9 May 2007.

ON RUNNING A STORY ABOUT THE CALL GIRL WHO BROUGHT DOWN JOHN PROFUMO, THE THEN-SECRETARY OF STATE FOR WAR.

People can sneer as much as they like, but I'll take the hundred fifty thousand extra copies we're going to sell.

— *MURDOCH: THE MAKING OF A MEDIA EMPIRE*, 1997.

ON NEWSPAPER SNOBS.

I'm not ashamed of any of my papers at all and I'm rather sick of snobs that tell us that they're bad papers, snobs who only read papers that no one else wants. I doubt if they read many papers at all. And whereas on most issues they consider themselves liberals or radicals or something, they think they ought to be imposing their taste on everyone else in the community.

— *RUPERT MURDOCH: NEWS CORPORATION MAGNATE*, 2011.

ON TRADITION.

[T]he old lifestyle of reading a newspaper over breakfast is gone.

— MEDIA SUMMIT, 8 FEBRUARY 2007.

On great journalism.

What happens to print journalism in an age where consumers are increasingly being offered on-demand, interactive, news, entertainment, sports and classifieds via broadband on their computer screens, TV screens, mobile phones and handsets? The answer is that great journalism will always attract readers. The words, pictures and graphics that are the stuff of journalism have to be brilliantly packaged; they must feed the mind and move the heart. And, crucially, newspapers must give readers a choice of accessing their journalism in the pages of the paper or on websites such as Times Online or – and this is important – on any platform that appeals to them, mobile phones, hand-held devices, iPads, whatever. As I have said, newspapers may become news-sites.

— Lecture for the Worshipful Company of Stationers and Newspaper Makers, 13 March 2006.

ON THE DOGGED PERSISTENCE AND PROFESSIONALISM OF HIS EMPLOYEES.

Our new world is one of modern mass communication, phone and text, without limit. Democracy will be from the bottom up, not from the top down. Even so, a free society requires an independent press: turbulent ... enquiring ... bustling ... and free.

That's why our journalism is hard-driving and questioning of authority. And so are our journalists. Often, I have cause to celebrate editorial endeavour. Occasionally, I have had cause for regret.

Let me be clear: We will vigorously pursue the truth – and we will not tolerate wrongdoing.

— *THE GUARDIAN*, 21 OCTOBER 2010.

ON THE POTENTIAL OF PRINT.

Our print businesses, and especially newspapers – the historic heart of this company – continue to deliver value for our company and shareholders, in part by generating huge amounts of cash that fund and fulfill our strategy. Right now our print businesses have more total readers than they ever have, thanks to the Internet. The distinction that today seems to divide 'new' and 'old' media will prove illusory over time. In the meantime, we are investing in the future of these businesses.

— ANNUAL SHAREHOLDERS' ADDRESS, 20 OCTOBER 2006.

ON MAINTAINING THE LEAD DOG POSITION.

We believe the way to keep advertisers is to be number one in everything we do.

— SPEECH FOR BEAR STEARNS CONFERENCE, 11 MARCH 2008.

ON MASS APPEAL.

To Barbara Walters: Well, there's nothing wrong with talking to the masses. You know, William Shakespeare wrote for the masses. I think if he was writing today, he'd probably be the chief scriptwriter on *All in the Family* or *Dallas*. They'd certainly be a bit bawdier.

—MURDOCH: THE MAKING OF A MEDIA EMPIRE, 1997.

ON THE OLD AND NEW BROADCASTING PARADIGMS.

We sensed ten years ago that people watching television news felt alienated by the monolithic presentation of the news they were getting from the nightly news broadcasts or cable networks. We sensed that there was another way we could deliver the news – objectively, fairly, and faster-paced. And the result was the Fox News Channel, today America's number one cable news network.

— SPEECH FOR THE AMERICAN SOCIETY OF NEWSPAPER EDITORS, 13 APRIL 2005.

ON THE LIBERATING POWERS OF COMMUNICATION TECHNOLOGY.

Advances in the technology of communications have proved an unambiguous threat to totalitarian regimes. Fax machines enable dissidents to bypass state-controlled print media; direct-dial telephone makes it difficult for a state to control interpersonal voice communication; and satellite broadcasting makes it possible for information-hungry residents of many closed societies to bypass state-controlled television channels.

— SPEECH FOR NEWS CORP. ADVERTISERS, 1 SEPTEMBER 1993.

ON MEDIA FLOURISHING IN CHINA.

China has the potential not only to follow the examples of the US and the UK, but to improve upon those examples and achieve a level of success all its own. By developing a regulatory system that is both firm enough to ensure China's control over her emerging businesses and smart enough not to stifle those businesses' growth, China will create an exemplary media industry.

— SPEECH FOR THE PARTY SCHOOL OF THE CHINA COMMUNIST PARTY CENTRAL COMMITTEE, 9 OCTOBER 2003.

ON DEFENDING IDEAS IN A FREE SOCIETY.

In a free society, you do not succeed just by having the right ideas. You succeed by having the confidence to defend those ideas when they are under assault – and to see them through when the experts are counselling compromise.

— *THE GUARDIAN*, 21 OCTOBER 2010.

ON RM's USE OF MEDIA TO PEDDLE POLITICAL INFLUENCE.

As for using our political influence in our newspapers or television to favour investments, that is nonsense. As for the investment in the [Millennial] Dome, that was some sponsorship by Sky which all the rest of our newspapers attacked as ridiculous. We're not going to work in some monolithic way like that.

And as for China, that's absolutely not the case. You get the odd disaffected journalist who will say anything about anybody.

— TESTIMONY GIVEN TO THE US HOUSE COMMITTEE ON THE JUDICIARY, 8 MAY 2003.

ON BLOGGERS.

Now, it would certainly serve the interests of the powerful if professional journalists were muted – or replaced as navigators in our society by bloggers and bloviators.

Bloggers can have a social role – but that role is very different to that of the professional seeking to uncover facts, however uncomfortable.

— *THE GUARDIAN*, 21 OCTOBER 2010.

ON VIRTUOUS PUBLISHING AND A VIGOROUS PRESS.

The vigorous virtues [Margaret Thatcher] championed have been a guide for me in my life and in my business. It's fair to say that we have worked hard and taken huge risks along the way.

Many of the defining moments of my career have been in Britain. This includes fundamentally changing the newspaper industry in the 1980s – which has helped give us all the uniquely vigorous press we enjoy today.

— *THE GUARDIAN*, 21 OCTOBER 2010.

On responsibility.

The buck stops with the guy who signs the checks.

—Attributed to RM.

ON OWNERSHIP AFFECTING THE
EDITORIAL PRODUCT.

I try to keep in touch with the details ... I also look at the product daily. That doesn't mean you interfere, but it's important to occasionally to show the ability to be involved. It shows you understand what's happening.

— BBC NEWS ONLINE, 1 AUGUST 2007.

ON HAVING A STERLING REPUTATION.

Our reputation is more important than the last hundred million dollars.

— DIRECTOR OF FINANCE ONLINE, 5 JULY 2010.

ON BEING ASKED WHO WAS RESPONSIBLE FOR THE PHONE TAPPING.

The people that I trusted to run it, and then maybe the people they trusted. I worked with Mr Hinton for fifty-two years and I would trust him with my life.

— UNCORRECTED TRANSCRIPT OF ORAL EVIDENCE GIVEN BEFORE THE CULTURE, MEDIA AND SPORT SELECT COMMITTEE, 19 JULY 2011.

ON INDEPENDENT DECISION-MAKING.

You can't build a strong corporation with a lot of committees and a board that has to be consulted at every turn. You have to be able to make decisions on your own.

— *CNBC BUSINESS*, MARCH 2012.

ON EDUCATION.

But the big, underlying thing in Western society is education. If we're going to lose a lot of our manufacturing, as we will, as globalisation goes on, to people [who] are getting paid five bucks a day, in China or India, who are just as intelligent as we are and even more hard working, then our people, all our people – and I hope it will come out – must be better educated ...

— *THE SYDNEY MORNING HERALD*, 7 APRIL 2004.

ON BEING AN OUTSIDER OF THE FIRMLY ENTRENCHED BRITISH SYSTEM.

I just wasn't prepared to join the system ... Maybe I just have an inferiority complex about being an Australian. My wife accuses me of this sometimes. But you've got some money and you tend to send your kids to the school you can most afford; you join the old-school-tie system and you're going to be dragged into the so-called social establishment somehow. I never was. Just as we were being invited round to places we'd catch Lord Lambton in bed or something, and then we'd be barred from everything ... It's very difficult not at some point to be sucked into the establishment. The last thing I wanted was to be a bloody press lord. I think when people start taking knighthoods and peerages it really is telling the world you've sold out. I've never been offered one. Well, I've been offered a knighthood a few times but no, I wouldn't take one.

— *THE VILLAGE VOICE,* 1976.

ON FORMER CBS NEWS ANCHOR DAN RATHER'S NOTION THAT THE GOVERNMENT SHOULD BAIL OUT NEWSPAPERS.

I think he's talking rubbish ... and very dangerous rubbish. We don't want government money in that we want a free press. It's essential to the democracy that we have a free, and as far as possible, competitive press. Or competitive information industry, if you will. And you won't get that if you start having government dollars coming in.

— *UNCOMMON KNOWLEDGE*, 5 FEBRUARY 2010.

The World Wide Web

ON GOOGLE PASSING UP MYSPACE.

I like those guys, but there's a bit of arrogance. They could have bought MySpace three months before we did for half the price. They thought, 'It's nothing special. We can do that.'

— *WIRED*, JULY 2006.

ON THE URGENCY IN BUYING MYSPACE.

We decided we had to act fast, started looking, found Intermix, which owned MySpace, which was three days away from being acquired by Viacom. We went into a room and came out with the company.

— *BARRON'S* ONLINE, 28 MAY 2008.

On MySpace's potential.

When we bought MySpace, we thought it had great possibilities. We didn't realise it would grow as fast as it has, and of course it has given birth to imitators, which I guess they're calling Web 3.0, or whatever, and given rise to what you'd call social networking.

We got a big wake-up call from Facebook last year. We put a lot of new things in this year. You can't write off MySpace.

—*Esquire* online, 11 September 2008.

On MySpace's valuation.

You were all laughing at me for buying MySpace. What's that worth today? It's worth more than twenty times what we paid for it.

— Speech for Goldman Sachs Communacopia XVI Conference, 18 September 2007.

On risky dot-com acquisitions.

We have not spent a fraction of what all our competitors have lost in this area. We have slowed down and are slowing down. We have been very tentative and careful. In retrospect, we would have liked to have been even more so.

— News Corp. General Meeting, October 2000.

ON MYSPACE CHANGING WITH ITS NEW
CORPORATE OWNERSHIP.

There are about sixty Rupert Murdochs up there. People post me there. Some aren't polite. They feel they own MySpace and that the big corporation was going to come in and change it. Well, we haven't.

— BBC NEWS ONLINE, 1 AUGUST 2007.

ON WRITING OFF MYSPACE'S US$545 MILLION
NET LOSS.

Many questions and jokes about MySpace. Simple answer: we screwed up in every way possible, learned lots of valuable, expensive lessons.

— TWITTER, 29 JUNE 2011.

ON ACQUIRING INTERNET PROPERTIES.

Empowering the consumer through greater choice is exactly what this company strives to accomplish. And there's no greater medium of choice than the Internet. That's why we are so drawn to the opportunities and challenges it represents. This is a time of fundamental change. So with relatively modest and extremely well-targeted investments, we have this year formed a special Internet unit and acquired properties that have instantly delivered us tens of millions of new customers, and, in the process, begun a transformation of the company ... [W]e now have the most potent combination of relevant content and critical audience mass to forge a real and profit-able presence on the Web.

— NEWS CORP. PRESS RELEASE, 21 OCTOBER 2005.

ON STEVE JOBS'S IPAD.

I think this is the end of the laptop ... Here we have the man who invented the personal computer, then the laptop. He's now destroying them. That is an amazing life.

— PRESS CONFERENCE, 2 FEBRUARY 2011.

ON CONTEXT AND CONTENT.

It's funny, because Steve Jobs was in yesterday showing his new iPad. And I went through that with him again. I said, 'Look, you're going to invent all these things. And they're wonderful, brilliant, but they mean nothing if you haven't got content to put on them.' And he agreed completely.

— *UNCOMMON KNOWLEDGE*, 5 FEBRUARY 2010.

ON PAYING FOR CONTENT.

Any content. Books, anything at all. You just have to pay. That's the future ... Let's not talk about paper. The news industry spends a fortune in collecting the news. It needs to be paid for it. There is not enough advertising to go around. It's alright on cable television because it gets paid by the cable suppliers, money, which, of course, gets passed on to the public, as well as supplemented by some advertising; and it has to be the same with other forms of news.

We test marketed it and people, I think, understand that it's perfectly fair that they are going to pay for it. If it doesn't, the newspapers will go out of business. All newspapers. There is just not enough advertising to go around for all the sites on the Internet ... The availability doubles and triples every year, but the amount of real money goes up 10 or 15 per cent a year. The price of it keeps coming down.

— TECHCRUNCH.COM, 17 NOVEMBER 2009.

ON THE FUTURE OF NEWSPAPERS.

Can newspapers make money online? Sure. Can they make enough to replace what's going out? At the moment, with the Internet so competitive, so new and so cheap, the answer is no. But don't look at it as a newspaper – look at it as a journalistic enterprise. If you've got authority and trust, if you can make the news interesting, you'll survive.

— *WIRED*, JULY 2006.

ON TABLETS' DIGITAL INK AND ECOLOGY.

There's going to be tens of millions of these things sold all over the world. It may be the saving of newspapers because you don't have the costs of paper, ink, printing, trucks. It doesn't destroy the traditional newspaper, it just comes in a different form.

— IBTIMES.COM, 2 FEBRUARY 2011.

ON NOT BUYING AOL AFTER MICROSOFT CO-FOUNDER BILL GATES DISSUADED HIM.

We had an opportunity to come in when it was four or five billion, and it went up to being worth $150 billion. It was a pretty serious opportunity that we missed there.

— *CLASH OF THE TITANS*, 2003.

ON INVESTING IN THE INTERNET.

There is no greater priority for the company today than to meaningfully and profitably expand its Internet presence and to properly position ourselves to benefit from the explosion in broadband usage that we are now starting to see.

— CONFERENCE CALL WITH ANALYSTS, 10 AUGUST 2005.

On monetising search engines and news aggregators.

We were outspoken. And we'll be more outspoken on the whole issue of payment for copyright material, and that goes to every aggregator, whether it be Yahoo! or Google or Ask.com or anything. We employ thousands and thousands of people as do others. I mean, there are billions of dollars spent, probably every month, but certainly every year in the collection and the creation of copyright by organisations and they cannot do that and have that material which they own stolen from them, or the business will be destroyed.

— THESTREET.COM, 2 JULY 2009.

ON NEWS CORP.'S GOAL.

The Internet is a great leveller. All newspapers count for less these days. So ... as far as I'm concerned, I want to drive News Corp., as I've said, into being the greatest content company, whether it's in news, opinions, writing or whether it be film or television. I mean there are so many new pipes in how you deliver these things. And so on. We'll just have to use them all and see what's economical. I had a study done, and I think you've had more studies done down there. What if they made *The Wall Street Journal* free instead of charging eighty bucks?

— *THE WALL STREET JOURNAL* ONLINE, 6 JUNE 2007.

On Google.

We've got to find new ways and new business models to get revenues. Or else the world is going to be owned by Google. I was asked at this investment thing I had to go to, what competitors I see I would have in five years' time. Globally. I said I'm sure there'll be a lot of them. I know one is Google. It's just getting so strong, so powerful. And I know the guys, and like them. They're friends of mine. But it is a big fact of life. They sort of just hit the mother lode of search advertising and they're just destroying Microsoft search, hurting Yahoo!'s and making others irrelevant. I don't understand the technologies but whatever their technology is, it seems to be producing a much higher margin of profit. What are they going to do next? I saw in *The New York Times* today they're devising ... a lot of computer applications which would directly challenge Microsoft, which they'll give away. So it's going to be very interesting. Four or five years ago we were all convinced Microsoft was going to take over the world. Now we're all convinced it's Google. But that's another subject.

— *The Wall Street Journal* online, 6 June 2007.

On the potential of the digital medium.

But the digital is a means, not an end. It is a mechanism by which people can transform their lives; to improve the education of their children; to reform health care; and, as we all know, to access news and information and entertainment on an unprecedented scale ... Media companies know that if you do not respond intelligently and creatively to the digital challenge, your future will be bleak indeed. The presses are now silent at some of the world's most famous newspapers – they were supposed to report on their societies, but somehow failed to notice that those societies were changing fundamentally.

— World Media Summit, 9 October 2009.

On traditional print's electronic evolution.

The Internet has been the most fundamental change during my lifetime and for hundreds of years. Someone the other day said, 'It's the biggest thing since Gutenberg', and then someone else said, 'No, it's the biggest thing since the invention of writing.'

— bytesdaily.blogspot.com, 11 July 2011.

ON THE WEB EMPOWERING PEOPLE.

To find something comparable, you have to go back five hundred years to the printing press, the birth of mass media – which, incidentally, is what really destroyed the old world of kings and aristocracies. Technology is shifting power away from the editors, the publishers, the establishment, the media elite. Now it's the people who are taking control … We're looking at the ultimate opportunity. The Internet is media's golden age.

— *WIRED*, JULY 2006.

ON CENSORING THE INTERNET.

All forms of government ultimately are not going to succeed in trying to control or censor the Internet. In China you can bar a certain word. But Google will still enable billions of people to get a great deal more knowledge and education, though it may not be political information. Still, all of that has to be good. China made a deliberate decision to let in the Internet. They felt it was necessary in joining the modern world. They are going to have to live with the consequences.

— THEDAILYBEAST.COM, 12 FEBRUARY 2006.

ON THE OFT-QUOTED MANTRA BY ONLINE PIRATES THAT 'INFORMATION WANTS TO BE FREE'.

There are many readers who believe that they are paying for content when they sign up with an internet service provider, presuming that they have bought a ticket to a content buffet. That misconception thrived on the silence of inarticulate institutions which were unable to challenge the fallacies and humbug of the e-establishment.

The value of content has been volatile in the past decade but we are entering another decisive phase in which device makers are again courting the creators of content. I have sensed that shift in recent days during my travels in Japan and South Korea where I met some of the world's leading electronics manufacturers. These companies don't want their customers to be served a diet of digital dross, and yet that will be the inevitable consequence if the worth of content and creativity are not appreciated.

The Philistine phase of the digital age is almost over. The aggregators and the plagiarists will soon have to pay a price for the co-opting of our content. But if we do not take advantage of the current movement toward paid-for content, it will be the content creators, the people in this hall, who pay the ultimate price and the content kleptomaniacs will triumph.

— WORLD MEDIA SUMMIT, 9 OCTOBER 2009.

ON CONTENT BEING KING.

THE NEWS CORPORATION IS ON THE CUSP OF A DIGITAL DYNASTY. CONTENT IS NOT JUST KING, IT IS THE EMPEROR.

— *UNCOMMON KNOWLEDGE*, 5 FEBRUARY 2010.

ON THE PROLIFERATION OF BROADBAND.

Most newspaper companies still have their heads in the sand, but other media companies are aggressive. And there are completely new start-up companies. There is a great pace of development, which is very exciting. At News Corp., we have been developing online extensions of traditional media for the last few years. What's happened now? We're seeing the spread of broadband. In the whole world today, only 190 million homes can receive broadband. That's going to go up in the next ten to twenty years to at least 3 billion homes. We're just now at the very beginning of the shift to digital media.

— THEDAILYBEAST.COM, 12 FEBRUARY 2006.

ON THE GENERATIONAL DIVIDE ON COMPUTERS.

I'm a digital immigrant. I wasn't weaned on the Web, nor coddled on a computer. Instead, I grew up in a highly centralised world where news and information were tightly controlled by a few editors. My two young daughters, on the other hand, will be digital natives. They'll never know a world without ubiquitous broadband Internet access.

— NEWS CORP. PRESS RELEASE, 13 APRIL 2005.

ON THE SPEED OF INFORMATION IN OUR DIGITAL AGE.

These are sophisticated individuals who will be role models for coming generations. Change moves swiftly in our digitally compressed age. The speed of information magnifies differences and highlights conflict. Yet I believe that the more we know about each other, the more we understand how much we have in common. And a free press is crucial to that process.

— ADDRESS AT THE YOMIUIRI INTERNATIONAL ECONOMIC SOCIETY, TOKYO, 6 NOVEMBER 2006.

Pronouncements
and Politics

ON THE IRAQ WAR.

Then-secretary of defence Donald Rumsfeld optimistically said it would be a very short war: 'I doubt six months.' Unfortunately, the war dragged on, spanning eight long years: I think what's important is that the world respects us, much more important than they love us ... There is going to be collateral damage. And if you really want to be brutal about it, better we get it done now than spread it over months ... It is very possible to see freelance suicide attempts both here and in London, and that would psychologically shake this country up.

— *THE GUARDIAN*, 3 APRIL 2003.

ON CHARGES THAT NEWS CORP. SHAPED THE IRAQ WAR'S AGENDA.

No, I don't think so. We tried ... We basically supported the Bush policy in the Middle East ... but we have been very critical of his execution.

— WORLD ECONOMIC FORUM, 26 JANUARY 2007.

ON THE US HOUSING BUBBLE.

It's very easy to blame the free market, but how did we get the housing bubble? We got it because of Congress pushing Fannie Mae and Freddie Mac into lending money to people who couldn't afford it and blowing up the price of housing; a Fed which was too loose with the money. It just led to this very naturally. When you get a bubble, it has to be lanced and it's painful. That's what we're going through.

— INTERVIEW ON FOX BUSINESS NETWORK, 28 APRIL 2009.

ON *THE NEW YORK TIMES* FAVOURING PRESIDENT OBAMA.

I have great respect for the *Times*, except that it does have an agenda: anything Mr Obama wants. You can see it. You can see it in that the White House pays them off by feeding them stories and so on.

— HUFFINGTONPOST.COM, 6 JUNE 2010.

ON GOVERNMENT REGULATION AND THE FREE MARKET.

Whether we like it or not, there's going to be increased regulation, and the government inserting a lot of taxpayer money into business. It's inevitable that they're going to play a bigger part. We have to accept it. On the other hand, we also have to agree that outside of that, we want to avoid over-regulating. We've got to stay believing in the free market system.

— INTERVIEW ON FOX BUSINESS NETWORK, 28 APRIL 2009.

ON RECESSION AND THE OBAMA ADMINISTRATION.

We have a huge deficit now. We're printing money, borrowing money. We can't do any more of either without having a run on the dollar ... which would cause a deeper recession. The president and the administration are caught in a trap, somewhat of their own making. They certainly can't do a second stimulus.

— WALLSTREETPIT.COM, 19 NOVEMBER 2009.

On political yin and yang in China.

There are human rights abuses in this country [US] too. The Chinese government is about keeping China together – they're nationalists in that sense. While they're doing this, I think they're very frightened of any organised dissent.

If you go to a Chinese home today, you will hear criticism of Chinese policy, government, or open discussion, which you certainly didn't get seven, eight years ago. On the other hand, if you want to go up the street and find someone on a soapbox making a speech, you won't. They'll be very quickly moved on. But I'd say it's much freer. Much more open than it was for the average citizen. But because they think their job above all else is to keep China together – remember over the course of civilisation they've been broken up, conquered and messed around with many times, they['ve] got to keep it together. Therefore they're trying to keep very strict control over the media and what goes out over television channels. I think they're getting a little looser about that, but I couldn't say radically.

— *The Murdoch Mission: The digital transformation of a media empire*, 2002.

ON CHINA CURIOUSLY BEREFT OF COMMUNISM.

I don't think there are many Communists left in China. There's a one-party state and there's a communist economy, which they are desperately trying to get out of and change ... The Chinese have had some border disputes, which one can argue about and I don't know the rights and wrongs of. I don't know the rights and wrongs of Tibet.

— *VANITY FAIR*, OCTOBER 1999.

ON CHINA'S 'OPEN DOOR'.

Without the 'open door' policy, China would still be an inward-looking, underdeveloped country whose talented people were far from fulfilling their potential. In the past three decades China has reclaimed its greatness by reopening itself to the world. It is a vivid example of why we must ensure that the nations of the world are open to business and open to each other.

— ADDRESS AT THE YOMIURI INTERNATIONAL ECONOMIC SOCIETY, TOKYO, 6 NOVEMBER 2006.

On Chinese repression of the news.

Is freedom of the press the privilege of a few countries or the right of all? Should the flow of information on the Internet be blocked? And who should do the blocking? Can a barricade be built against the world outside? As Asia has developed, there has been a vigorous debate about values. Some have argued that the West has tried to impose its values on this region … [A] free press also holds companies, governments and individuals to account. Accountability is not a Western value. It is a necessary condition for success.

> — Address at the Yomiuri International Economic
> Society, Tokyo, 6 November 2006.

ON THE CONTRAST BETWEEN CHINA AND INDIA IN THE FLOW OF INFORMATION.

There is a vigorous debate about the relative strengths and weaknesses of China and India. But one fact is beyond debate. The free flow of information is a crucial advantage in an ultra-competitive world. There is no doubt that India is producing thousands of managers who are capable of running any company anywhere in the world. There is also no doubt that these impressive managers would not be developed in such impressive numbers if India attempted to dam the flow of facts or opinion.

— ADDRESS AT THE YOMIUIRI INTERNATIONAL ECONOMIC
SOCIETY, TOKYO, 6 NOVEMBER 2006.

On the byzantine Chinese market.

We don't do very well in China. We have an interest. We just sold half of it in Phoenix Television ... We have got five times our money back of our total investment and we are still there. We brought on a new partner, China Mobile, and this has been a very good base and we think it will do nicely. And we have our own little channel, Xing Kong, which is produced in Shanghai and distributed through the southeast. That's pretty much a break-even operation.

We are very modest. All I would say there is that nobody – and I challenge anyone to argue this – nobody, none of the American media companies or British media companies have made any impact there yet. There may be a MySpace China which has been licensed but we are just feeling our way there ... It's a vast market, but it's certainly a very, very sensitive one ... It is a very difficult market for outsiders.

— INDIANTELEVISION.COM, 8 February 2007.

On patience with China.

China is vast, but China has not opened up yet. We keep a presence there. We're going to behave ourselves and be there until we see a change in policies. And it will have to come. It's a sovereign country, and that's the way they do things, and we'll just wait.

— Media event, 8 February 2007.

On China lowering the bamboo curtain.

A year ago I would have said there's a lot of opening up going on. The present trend is the reverse. The authorities are now quite paranoid about what gets through.

— Media conference, 16 September 2005.

ON ESTABLISHING A MEDIA FOOTHOLD IN CHINA.

News Corporation is very keen to explore opportunities for cooperation in China, based of course on respect and understanding of China's unique cultural and social values. Of course, my company has much to learn about doing business in China and we have made some mistakes.

— MEETING WITH DING GUANGEN, BEIJING, 24 OCTOBER 1997.

ON CHINA EMBRACING NEW TECHNOLOGIES.

China has proved the skeptics, including myself, wrong, by not shunning new information technologies, but embracing them ... Advances in telecommunications contribute to the 'universalisation' of cultural interests and lifestyles. However, nations retain their own social and moral values that the media must take into account. China is a distinctive market with distinctive social and moral values that Western companies must learn to abide by.

— KEYNOTE ADDRESS, 15 MAY 1997.

THE IRAQ WAR

**WE CAN'T BACK DOWN NOW, WHERE YOU HAND
OVER THE WHOLE OF THE MIDDLE EAST TO
SADDAM ... I THINK BUSH IS ACTING VERY
MORALLY, VERY CORRECTLY, AND I THINK HE
IS GOING TO GET ON WITH IT.**

— *THE GUARDIAN*, 16 FEBRUARY 2003.

ON OPTIMISM, OIL, AND THE IRAQ WAR.

Who knows what the future holds? I have a pretty optimistic medium- and long-term view but things are going to be pretty sticky until we get Iraq behind us. But once it's behind us, the whole world will benefit from cheaper oil which will be a greater stimulus than anything else.

— *THE GUARDIAN*, 11 FEBRUARY 2003.

. . . .

On the belief that cheap oil at $20 a barrel would be an outcome of war with Iraq. (As of April 2012, the price was $122.34 for a barrel of Brent Crude Oil, according to oil-price.net.): The greatest thing to come out of this for the world economy, if you could put it that way, would be $20 a barrel for oil. That's bigger than any tax cut in any country.

— *THE GUARDIAN*, 11 FEBRUARY 2003.

ON PM TONY BLAIR'S SUPPORT OF PRESIDENT GEORGE BUSH'S IRAQ WAR.

I think Tony is being extraordinarily courageous and strong on what his stance is in the Middle East. It's not easy to do that living in a party which is largely composed of people that have a knee-jerk anti-Americanism and are sort of pacifist. But he's shown great guts, as he did, I think, in Kosovo and over various problems in the old Yugoslavia.

— *THE GUARDIAN,* 16 FEBRUARY 2003.

ON HIS REPUTED POWER ON CAPITOL HILL.

Power? What power? I have no power. No more than any American. This myth that I have some influence up there on Capitol Hill is baloney.

— *CLASH OF THE TITANS,* 2003.

ON COVERAGE OF WATERGATE AND RICHARD NIXON, WHOM HE SUPPORTED.

I differ from the vast majority of my peers in this country in that I believe the new cult of adversarial journalism has sometimes been taken to the point of subversion. It is a disgrace that we can and do read thousands upon thousands of words about our national defence and our foreign policy every day without so much as a nod of recognition to the enormous risks to our freedom that exist today – to the terrifying consequences of Russian and Cuban bases on this continent ... It is a sorry fact that the media as a whole ... unquestioningly embrace a welfare state which divides and embitters our society without helping the truly poor and needy.

— *MURDOCH: THE MAKING OF A MEDIA EMPIRE*, 1997.

On the cost of bucking
the establishment.

**Sometimes you're treated like
the skunk at a tea party. But
that's the fate of anyone who
challenges the status quo.**

— *Clash of the Titans*, 2003.

Phone-hacking

**ON MURDERED 13-YEAR-OLD MILLY DOWLER,
WHOSE PHONE WAS HACKED, GIVING HER PARENTS
FALSE HOPE THAT SHE WAS STILL ALIVE.**

I was absolutely shocked, appalled and ashamed when I heard about the Milly Dowler case only two weeks ago.

— *The Sydney Morning Herald*, 20 July 2011.

....

The settlement to Dowler's parents alone cost Murdoch £3.2 million, with additional, costly settlements made to other aggrieved parties. This apologia for tapping Milly Dowler's phone was also printed: We are sorry.

The News of the World was in the business of holding others to account. It failed when it came to itself.

We are sorry for the serious wrongdoing that occurred.

We are deeply sorry for the hurt suffered by the individuals affected.

We regret not acting faster to sort things out.

I realise that simply apologising is not enough.

Our business was founded on the idea that a free and open press should be a positive force in society. We need to live up to this.

In the coming days, as we take further concrete steps to resolve these issues and make amends for the damage they have caused, you will hear from us.

— *USA Today* ONLINE, 15 July 2011.

ON THE PHONE-HACKING SCANDAL.

We have very strict rules. There was an incident more than five years ago. The person who bought a bugged phone conversation was immediately fired and in fact he subsequently went to jail. There have been two parliamentary inquiries, which have found no further evidence or any other thing at all. If anything was to come to light, we challenge people to give us evidence, and no one has been able to. If any evidence comes to light, we will take immediate action like we took before.

— THE MAYNE REPORT, 15 OCTOBER 2010.

ON HOW NEWS CORP. HANDLED THE PHONE-HACKING SCANDAL.

[M]inor mistakes.

— *FINANCIAL TIMES*, 14 July 2011.

The Wall Street Journal's vigorous defence of its boss.

Phone-hacking is illegal, and it is up to British authorities to enforce their laws. If Scotland Yard failed to do so adequately when the hacking was first uncovered several years ago, then that is more troubling than the hacking itself ... We also trust that our readers can see through the commercial and ideological motives of our competitor-critics. The schadenfreude is so thick you can't cut it with a chainsaw ... In braying for politicians to take down Mr Murdoch and News Corp., our media colleagues might also stop to ask about possible precedents.

— *The Wall Street Journal*, 18 July 2011.

ON *NEWS OF THE WORLD* PERMANENTLY
SUSPENDING PUBLICATION.

Wrongdoers turned a good newsroom bad and this was not fully understood or adequately pursued. As a result, the *News of the World* and News International wrongly maintained that these issues were confined to one reporter ... The paper made statements to parliament without being in the full possession of the facts. This was wrong. The company paid out-of-court settlements approved by me. I now know that I did not have a complete picture when I did so. This was wrong and is a matter of serious regret ... Having consulted senior colleagues, I have decide that we must take further decisive action with respect to the paper. This Sunday will be the last issue of the *News of the World*.

— BBC NEWS ONLINE, 7 JULY 2011.

BACKING REBEKAH BROOKS, *NEWS OF THE WORLD* EDITOR.

I have made clear that our company must fully and proactively cooperate with the police in all investigations and that is exactly what News International has been doing and will continue to do under Rebekah Brooks' leadership.

— REUTERS Edition US, 6 July 2011.

ON *NEWS OF THE WORLD* EDITOR REBEKAH BROOKS'S ADMISSION OF WRONGDOING GIVEN AT A PARLIAMENTARY HEARING.

I didn't know of it, I'm sorry. Allow me to say something? This is not an excuse. Maybe it is an explanation of my laxity. The *News of the World* is less than 1 per cent of our company. I employ 53,000 people around the world who are proud and great and ethical and distinguished people – professionals in their line. Perhaps I am spread [too thin] watching and appointing people whom I trust to run those divisions.

— UNCORRECTED TRANSCRIPT OF ORAL EVIDENCE GIVEN BEFORE THE CULTURE, MEDIA AND SPORT SELECT COMMITTEE, 19 JULY 2011.

On all the criticism.

**[J]ust getting annoyed.
I'll get over it. I'm tired.**

— *The Wall Street Journal*, 14 July 2011.

ON CREDIBILITY WITH HIS
NEWSPAPER'S READERSHIP.

[T]he important point was that we had broken our trust with
our readers.

— UNCORRECTED TRANSCRIPT OF ORAL EVIDENCE GIVEN BEFORE
THE CULTURE, MEDIA AND SPORT SELECT COMMITTEE,
19 JULY 2011.

ON POTENTIAL FALLOUT TO THE COMPANY
BECAUSE OF THE PHONE-HACKING SCANDAL.

[N]othing that will not be recovered. We have a reputation of
great good works in this country.

— THE WALL STREET JOURNAL, 14 JULY 2011.

On the launch of *The Sun*.

The Sun *was launched against the backdrop of arrests: nine of its journalists and executives, past and present, were being investigated over alleged payments to corrupt police and public officials*: We will obey the law. Illegal activities cannot and will not be tolerated – at any of our publications. Our Board of Directors, our management team and I take these issues very seriously.

We are doing everything we can to assist those who were arrested – all suspensions are hereby lifted until or whether charged and they are welcome to return to work. News Corporation will cover their legal expenses. Everyone is innocent unless proven otherwise.

I made a commitment last summer that I would do everything I could to get to the bottom of our problems and make this company an example to Fleet Street of ethical journalism. We will continue to ensure that all appropriate steps are taken to protect legitimate journalistic privilege and sources, which I know are essential for all of you to do your jobs. But we cannot protect people who have paid public officials.

— A note to the staff of News Corp., 17 February 2012.

ON ACCOUNTABILITY OF NEWS CORP. IN THE
WAKE OF ITS SYSTEMIC PHONE-TAPPING SCANDAL.

As has been widely publicised, our company has received a major black eye from the phone-hacking scandal at our *News of the World* newspaper in the UK. As I said at a parliamentary hearing, this episode has been the most humbling of my career.

Let me be clear: the behaviour carried out by some employees of *News of the World* is unacceptable and does not represent who we are as a company. It went against everything that I stand for. That behaviour betrayed not only our readers, but also the many thousands of magnificent professionals in every one of our other divisions around the world. It was a painful decision to shut down the *News of the World*, but it was the right thing to do.

As I write this letter, our Board of Directors and senior management are acting decisively to get to the bottom of what happened. I have asked Joel Klein, who formerly served in the US Justice Department, to lead our efforts in this matter. He reports to independent director Viet Dinh, who in turn is having regular meetings with all the other independent directors. The Board of Directors and the company have retained independent counsel, and we are cooperating with the relevant authorities in both the UK and the US. In sum, we have taken decisive actions to hold people accountable – and we will do whatever is necessary to prevent something like this from ever occurring again. We will put things right.

— NEWS CORP. ANNUAL REPORT, 2011.

News Corp.'s apology for hacking celebrities' phones.

Following an extensive internal investigation and disclosures through civil legal cases, News International has decided to approach some civil litigants with an unreserved apology and an admission of liability in cases meeting specific criteria.

We have also asked out lawyers to establish a compensation scheme with a view to dealing with justifiable claims fairly and efficiently.

This will begin the process of bringing these cases to a fair resolution with damages appropriate to the extent of the intrusion.

We will, however, continue to contest cases that we believe are without merit or where we are not responsible.

That said, past behaviour at the *News of the World* in relation to voicemail interception is a matter of genuine regret.

It is now apparent that our previous inquiries failed to uncover important evidence and we acknowledge our actions then were not sufficiently robust.

We continue to co-operate fully with the Metropolitan Police. It was our discovery and voluntary disclosure of this evidence in January that led to the reopening of the police investigation.

With that investigation ongoing, we cannot comment further until its completion.

— News International statement, 11 April 2011.

On betrayal, to the British Parliament on the phone hacking scandal.

I feel that the people I trusted ... I'm not saying who ... let me down and I think they behaved disgracefully. And it's time for them to pay.

— NPR, 19 July 2011.

CLOSING STATEMENT TO THE CULTURE, MEDIA
AND SPORT SELECT COMMITTEE.

Thank you, Mr Chairman. Members of the Committee, I would like to read a short statement now. My son and I came here with great respect for all of you, for Parliament and for the people of Britain, whom you represent. This is the most humble day of my career. After all that has happened, I know that we needed to be here today. James and I would like to say how sorry we are for what has happened, especially with regard to listening to the voicemail of victims of crime.

My company has 52,000 employees. I have led it for fifty-seven years, and I have made my share of mistakes. I have lived in many countries, employed thousands of honest and hard-working journalists. I own nearly 200 newspapers of very different sizes and have followed countless stories about people and families around the world. At no time do I remember being as sickened as when I heard what the Dowler family had to endure – which I think was last Monday week – nor do I recall being as angry as when I was told that the *News of the World* could have compounded their distress. I want to thank the Dowlers for graciously giving me the opportunity to apologise in person.

I would like all the victims of phone hacking to know how completely and deeply sorry I am. Apologising cannot take back what has happened. Still, I want them to know the depth of my regret for the horrible invasions into their lives. I fully understand their ire, and I intend to work tirelessly to merit their forgiveness.

I understand our responsibility to co-operate with today's session as well as with future inquiries. We now know that things went badly wrong at the *News of the World*. For a newspaper that held others to account, it failed when it came to itself. The behaviour that occurred went against everything that I stand for – and my son, too. It not only betrayed our readers and me, but also the many thousands of magnificent professionals in other divisions of our company around the world. Let me be clear in saying: invading people's privacy by listening to their voicemail is wrong; paying police officers for information is wrong. They are inconsistent with our codes of conduct and neither has any place in any part of the company that I run.

But saying sorry is not enough. Things must be put right. No excuses. This is why News International is co-operating fully with the police, whose job it is to see that justice is done. It is our duty not to prejudice the outcome of the legal process. I am sure the Committee will understand this. I wish that we had managed to see and fully solve these problems much earlier. When two men were sent to prison in 2007, I thought this matter had been settled. The police ended their investigations, and I was told that News International conducted an internal review. I am confident that when James later rejoined News

Corporation, he thought the case had closed, too. These are subjects you will no doubt wish to explore, and have explored today.

This country has given me, our companies and our employees many opportunities. I am grateful for them. I hope our contribution to Britain will one day also be recognised. Above all, I hope that we will come to understand the wrongs of the past, prevent them from happening again and, in the years ahead, restore the nation's trust in our company and in all British journalism. I am committed to doing everything in my power to make this happen. Thank you.

— UNCORRECTED TRANSCRIPT OF ORAL EVIDENCE GIVEN BEFORE
THE CULTURE, MEDIA AND SPORT SELECT COMMITTEE,
19 JULY 2011.

For better or for worse, our company is a reflection of my thinking, my character, my values.

—ATTRIBUTED TO RM.

Timeline

In its annual report for 2011, News Corporation, under Investor Operations, lists six industry segments: 'cable network programming; filmed entertainment; television; direct broadcast satellite television; publishing; and other. The activities of News Corp. are conducted principally in the United States, Continental Europe, the United Kingdom, Australia, Asia, and Latin America.'

The report states that News Corp.'s annual revenue is US$34 billion and its assets are estimated at US$60 billion.

News Corp. operates in over 800 companies in over fifty countries.

1931

Keith Rupert Murdoch is born in Melbourne, Australia, to Sir Keith Murdoch and Elisabeth Greene. RM has three sisters but no brothers. (11 March.)

1941

RM is admitted to Geelong Grammar, a prestigious boarding school in Australia, where he gets his first taste of publishing: he co-edits *The Corian*, the school's official journal, and edits the student journal, *If Revived*.

1949

RM graduates from Geelong Grammar.

1950

RM is admitted to Worcester College, Oxford University, where he reads Philosophy, Politics and Economics.

1952

RM's father, Sir Keith Murdoch, dies; RM inherits News Limited, the family business. He starts his newspaper career as publisher of the *Adelaide News*. In his will, Sir Keith Murdoch wrote, '... I desire that my said son Keith

Rupert Murdoch should have the great opportunity of spending a useful altruistic and full life in newspaper and broadcasting activities and of ultimately occupying a position of high responsibility in that field with the support of my trustees if they consider him worthy of that support ...'. (4 October.)

1953

RM graduates from Worcester College with an MA degree.

RM apprentices himself for six months under Lord Beaverbrook who practises 'the Black Art of journalism' at the *Daily Express* in London. Beaverbrook drills in him the benefits of independent newspapers. Beaverbrook tells him, 'If you work for me, you will never become a millionaire, but you will live like one.'

In September RM takes his father's place, inheriting the mantle of publisher of News Limited.

1955

RM merges two rival newspapers, the *Sunday Mail* and the *Advertiser.*

1956

RM marries Patricia Booker. (1 March.)

1958

RM and Patricia Murdoch's first child, Prudence, is born. (12 August.)

RM buys Channel 9 in Adelaide.

1960

RM buys the Sydney tabloid *The Daily Mirror*.

1962

RM buys Channel WIN 4 based in Wollongong, New South Wales.

1963

RM buys part interest in Asia Magazines Ltd.

1964

RM buys *Dominion*, a New Zealand newspaper, and starts up *The Australian*.

1967

RM divorces Patricia Murdoch.

RM marries Anna Torv. (28 April.)

1968

RM and Anna Murdoch's first child, Elisabeth, is born.
(22 August.)

1969

RM gains controlling shares of *News of the World*,
a London paper.

RM buys London broadsheet *The Sun*.

1971

RM and Anna Murdoch's first son, Lachlan, is born.
(8 September.)

1972

RM and Anna's second son, James, is born.
(13 December.)

1973

RM moves to San Antonio, Texas, and acquires the *San Antonio Express-News*. He later moves his family to New York.

1974

RM begins publishing the *National Star*, a national US newspaper.

1976

RM buys two US publications: the *New York Post* and *New York Magazine*.

1979

RM buys controlling shares of two companies: United Telecasters Ltd and Ansett Transport Industries.

Creates News Corporation as a holding company for News Limited.

1981

RM buys two papers in the UK: *The Times*, a London broadsheet, and the *Sunday Times*, a national UK broadsheet.

1982

RM buys *The Boston Herald*.

1984

RM is awarded the Companion of the Order of Australia for 'service to the media, particularly the newspaper publishing industry'.

1985

News Corp. makes a public announcement that it will buy a half-interest in a US film company, Twentieth Century-Fox Film Corporation. (On 23 September, News Corp. buys the other half.)

News Corp. announces its deal to buy Metromedia TV stations.

RM becomes a naturalised US citizen and, under Australian law, automatically loses citizenship to his birth country. (RM elects to become a US citizen to facilitate business matters, as noncitizens are not allowed to buy US TV stations. His action prompts William Safire of the *New York Times* to write, 'Isn't it true that his main reason for becoming a citizen is simple greed and lust for power? ... Americans should remind him that allegiance means loyalty, sometimes passionate loyalty.')

1986

News Corp. is embroiled in a labour controversy when RM, in the name of modernisation, consolidates his printing operations in Wapping (London); it results in a controversial, bitter and ultimately costly labour dispute.

RM creates Fox Inc.

1987

Tycoon Robert Maxwell, poised to buy the British newspaper *Today*, unwisely tells RM his plans. RM buys it from under him for £38 million. By adding this fifth newspaper to his holdings, RM now owns one-third of all papers in the UK.

News Corp. is forced to sell the *New York Post* due to federal regulations regarding media cross-ownership after the purchase of TV station WNYW-TV.

1988

News Corp. makes public announcement regarding the launch of Sky Television.

1989

News Corp. acquires HarperCollins, a US book publishing company, one of the 'Big Six' publishers in New York City.

1990

News Corp. forms British Sky Broadcasting Group (BSkyB) by merging Sky Television and British Satellite Broadcasting.

News Corp. faces a major financial crisis when a small bank in Pittsburgh, Pennsylvania, refuses to roll over its loan of AU$10 million and demands immediate payment in full. The small bank is oblivious to the fact that News Corp. would be forced into involuntary bankruptcy.

1991

A consortium of banks, faced with the prospect of a major default by News Corp., agrees to rework the loans. The possibility of a catastrophic financial meltdown is narrowly averted.

1993

RM's then-magazine *New Idea* publishes the transcript of an illegally recorded phone conversation between

Prince Charles and his then-married mistress, Camilla
Parker Bowles, from a landline phone at Eaton Hall
in Cheshire. Unable to tamp down the controversy
surrounding what was dubbed 'Camillagate', Prince
Charles simply maintains a stiff upper lip. In the UK,
RM's *The Sun* runs the full transcript, doubling sales that
day to 1.3 million.

In a bid to acquire a 34 per cent interest in Hughes
Electronics Corporation, RM testifies before the
Committee on the Judiciary of the US House of
Representatives, explaining News Corp.'s views on
'Direct Broadcast Satellite Service in the Multichannel
Video Distribution Market'. When questioned about his
'political influence in our newspapers or television', RM
replied that it was 'nonsense'.

1996

News Corp.'s conservative Fox News takes to the air,
offering an alternative to CNN, a 24-hour news station.

1997

In an effort to expand his broadcasting into China,
RM travels to Beijing, where he meets Vice-Premier
Zhu Rongji.

1998

RM divorces Anna Murdoch.

1999

RM marries Wendi Deng. (25 June.)

2000

RM is diagnosed with prostate cancer at sixty-nine years of age. (His father died of the same disease at age sixty-seven.)

2003

RM buys a satellite TV company in the US, DirecTV, for US$6 billion.

RM publicly backs US President George Bush and UK Prime Minister Tony Blair for their support of the Iraq War.

2005

News Corp. buys Intermix Media Inc. for US$580 million, which owns social networking sites, including MySpace; also buys Imagine Games Network for US$650 million.

2007

News Corp. acquires Dow Jones for US$5 billion, a record purchase. RM now owns the prestigious *Wall Street Journal*, *Barron's* magazine, *Far Eastern Economic Review* magazine, *SmartMoney Magazine*, MarketWatch.com and two radio shows (*The Wall Street Journal Report*, and *The Dow Jones Report*).

2009

A longtime believer in paying for online access, RM announces that he will implement a pay-to-read-online policy for his newspapers.

2010

The Times and *The Sunday Times* begin charging for online access.

2011

News Corp.'s British tabloid *News of the World* is embroiled in a phone-hacking scandal with major repercussions. RM and his son James provide testimony to the UK legislature's Culture, Media and Sport Select Committee.

In the wake of the scandal, the 168-year-old tabloid shuts down permanently; its last headline said, simply, 'Thank you and goodbye.'

2012

RM agrees to an out-of-court settlement, worth millions of pounds, with nineteen high-profile victims of the *News of the World*'s phone-hacking.

RM's son James, chairman of satellite broadcaster BSkyB, resigns in the wake of the phone-hacking scandal.

The British House of Commons Culture, Media and Sport Committee finds RM 'not a fit person to exercise the stewardship of a major international company'.

Sources

ON BEING OSTRACISED AT GEELONG GRAMMAR.

William Shawcross, *Murdoch: The making of a media empire*
(New York: Simon & Schuster, 1997).

ON HIS FATHER.

'Rupert Murdoch Has Potential', *Esquire* online,
11 September 2008.
'Uncorrected Transcript of Oral Evidence to be published as
HC 903-ii: House of Commons/oral evidence taken before the
culture, media and sport select committee/Phone Hacking/
Tuesday 19 July 2011/Rupert Murdoch and James Murdoch/
Rebekah Brooks', London, House of Commons Information
Office, prepared 25 July 2011, published online at www.
parliament.uk.

ON BEING A POLARISING PUBLIC FIGURE.

'Rupert Murdoch Has Potential', *Esquire* online,
11 September 2008.

ON IMMORTALITY.

Media Summit, sponsored by The McGraw-Hill Companies,
New York City, 8 February 2007. Interviewed by *Bloomberg
Businessweek* editor Steve Adler.

ON BEING A NORMAL PERSON.

'Rupert Murdoch Has Potential', *Esquire* online,
11 September 2008.

ON HIS TECH SHORTCOMINGS.

Richard Hack, *Clash of the Titans* (Beverly Hills, Ca.: New
Millennium Press, 2003).

ON CONSTANTLY MOVING FORWARD.

'Rupert Murdoch Has Potential', *Esquire* online,
11 September 2008.

ON HIS LEGACY.

William Shawcross, 'Murdoch's New Life', *Vanity Fair*,
October 1999.

ON WORKING WITH HIS CHILDREN.

'Rupert Murdoch Has Potential', *Esquire* online,
11 September 2008.

ON HIS SONS.

'Rupert Murdoch Has Potential', *Esquire* online,
11 September 2008.

ON NEPOTISM.

'Uncorrected Transcript of Oral Evidence to be published as
HC 903-ii: House of Commons/oral evidence taken before
the culture, media and sport select committee/Phone
Hacking/Tuesday 19 July 2011/Rupert Murdoch and James
Murdoch/Rebekah Brooks', London, House of Commons
Information Office, prepared 25 July 2011, published online
at www.parliament.uk.

ON HIS DAUGHTER ELISABETH'S EDUCATION.

Michael Wolff, 'The Secrets of His Succession', *Vanity Fair*,
December 2008.

ON AUSTRALIA AS HIS HOME BASE.

William Shawcross, *Murdoch: The making of a media empire* (New York: Simon & Schuster, 1997).

ON THE BREAKDOWN OF HIS SECOND MARRIAGE.

William Shawcross, 'Murdoch's New Life', *Vanity Fair*, October 1999.

ON HIS WANDERING HEART.

Michael Wolff, 'Tuesdays with Rupert', *Vanity Fair*, October 2008.

ON WENDI DENG.

Michael Wolff, 'The Secrets of His Succession', *Vanity Fair*, December 2008.
Mark Russell, 'Murdoch on Wendi', www.newser.com, 22 July 2011.

ON PRESIDENT GEORGE BUSH AND THE IRAQ WAR.

'Murdoch Backs "Courageous" Blair over Iraq', *The Guardian*, 11 February 2003.

ON BARACK OBAMA.

Hilary Rosen, 'Rupert Murdoch Says Obama Will Win', www.huffingtonpost.com, 29 May 2008.
Max Suich, 'Uncut: The thoughts of Chairman Murdoch', *Financial Review* online, 5 November 2010.
Danny Shea, 'Rupert Murdoch ...' www.huffingtonpost.com, 7 July 2009.
Rupert Murdoch, Twitter, 15 January 2012.

ON THEN-SENATOR HILARY CLINTON AS A PRESIDENTIAL CANDIDATE.

Media Summit, sponsored by The McGraw-Hill Companies, New York City, 8 February 2007. Interviewed by *Bloomberg Businessweek* editor Steve Adler.

ON FORMER HOUSE SPEAKER NEWT GINGRICH AS A PRESIDENTIAL CANDIDATE.

Media Summit, sponsored by The McGraw-Hill Companies, New York City, 8 February 2007. Interviewed by *Bloomberg Businessweek* editor Steve Adler.

ON NEW YORK MAYOR MICHAEL BLOOMBERG AS PRESIDENT.

Media Summit, sponsored by The McGraw-Hill Companies, New York City, 8 February 2007. Interviewed by *Bloomberg Businessweek* editor Steve Adler.

ON ARIZONA SENATOR JOHN MCCAIN'S RUN FOR PRESIDENCY.

Hilary Rosen, 'Rupert Murdoch Says Obama Will Win', www.huffingtonpost.com, 29 May 2008.

ON CNN COMMENTATOR GLENN BECK.

Max Suich, 'Uncut: The thoughts of Chairman Murdoch', *Financial Review* online, 5 November 2010.

ON CONSERVATIVE FOX NEWS ANCHOR BILL O'REILLY.

Max Suich, 'Uncut: The thoughts of Chairman Murdoch', *Financial Review* online, 5 November 2010.

ON THE WELL-REGARDED OFFICIAL STEVE JOBS BIOGRAPHY BY WALTER ISAACSON.

Rupert Murdoch, Twitter, 3 January 2012.

ON MEDIA MOGUL TED TURNER.

Wendy Goldman Rohm, *The Murdoch Mission: The digital transformation of a media empire,* (New York: John Wiley & Sons, 2002).

ON CAMILLAGATE.

'Camillagate Scoop Raises Questions for Murdoch', *The Sydney Morning Herald*, 31 July 2011.

On former prime minister Margaret Thatcher.

'Rupert Murdoch's Margaret Thatcher Lecture',
The Guardian, 21 October 2010.
Michael Leapman, *Arrogant Aussie: The Rupert Murdoch story*
(New York: Lyle Stuart, Inc., 1985).

On former prime minister Tony Blair.

Fran Abrams and Anthony Bevins, 'Murdoch's Courtship of
Blair Finally Pays Off', The Independent, 11 February 1998.
'Blair Saw Anti-American Bias in BBC News, Murdoch Says',
Agence-France Presse, 17 September 2005.

On Judith Regan.

Media Summit, sponsored by The McGraw-Hill Companies,
New York City, 8 February 2007. Interviewed by *Bloomberg
Businessweek* editor Steve Adler.

On Italian prime minister Silvio Berlusconi.

Hilary Rosen, 'Rupert Murdoch Says Obama Will Win',
www.huffingtonpost.com, 29 May 2008.

On Robert Maxwell.

Adam Curtis, 'Rupert Murdoch – A Portrait of Satan',
www.bbc.co.uk, 30 January 2011.

On Tibet.

William Shawcross, 'Murdoch's New Life', *Vanity Fair*,
October 1999.

On printer's ink in his blood.

Michael Leapman, *Arrogant Aussie: The Rupert Murdoch story*
(New York: Lyle Stuart, Inc., 1985).

On tabloids.

Eric Pooley, 'Exclusive: Rupert Murdoch speaks', *Time*, 28
June 2007.

On the *Adelaide News*'s libel charge.

Michael Leapman, *Arrogant Aussie: The Rupert Murdoch story* (New York: Lyle Stuart, Inc., 1985).

On most newspapers' failure to keep up with digital technologies.

Johnnie L Roberts, 'Murdoch's New Groove', www.thedailybeast.com, 12 February 2006.

On the challenges of working with newspaper editors.

Michael Leapman, *Arrogant Aussie: The Rupert Murdoch story* (New York: Lyle Stuart, Inc., 1985).

On the future of print newspapers.

Eric Savitz, 'D: News Corp.'s Murdoch "mystified" by YHOO's failure to do MSFT deal; sees recession; will he vote for Obama?', *Barron's* online, 28 May 2008.

On the power of newspapers.

Alex Gallafent, 'Rupert Murdoch through the Years', www.theworld.org, 14 July 2011.

On newspapers taking on debt.

David Kaplan, 'Murdoch: Newspapers must charge for online; debt is the problem, not print', www.paidcontent.org, 28 May 2009.

On suffering cash flow problems.

William Shawcross, *Murdoch: The making of a media empire* (New York: Simon & Schuster, 1997).

After the bank crisis was resolved in the *News*'s favour.

William Shawcross, *Murdoch: The making of a media empire* (New York: Simon & Schuster, 1997).

ON BUYING DOW JONES, WHICH OWNS *THE WALL STREET JOURNAL*.

Media Summit, sponsored by The McGraw-Hill Companies, New York City, 8 February 2007. Interviewed by *Bloomberg Businessweek* editor Steve Adler.

ON NEGOTIATIONS TO BUY *THE WALL STREET JOURNAL*.

Richard Siklos and Andrew Ross Sorkin, 'Murdoch on Owning *The Wall Street Journal*', *The New York Times*, 4 May 2007.

ON ACQUIRING *THE WALL STREET JOURNAL*.

Sarah Ellison, *War at* The Wall Street Journal: *Inside the struggle to control an American business empire* (New York: Houghton Mifflin Harcourt Publishing Company, 2010).

ON THE HIDDEN COST OF *THE WALL STREET JOURNAL*.

Eric Pooley, 'Exclusive: Rupert Murdoch speaks', *Time*, 28 June 2007.

ON HAVING BOUGHT *THE WALL STREET JOURNAL*.

'Rupert Murdoch Has Potential', *Esquire* online, 11 September 2008.

ON THE AFTERMATH OF NEWS CORP.'S ACQUISITION OF DOW JONES.

News Corp. press release, 1 August 2007.

AND WHEN THE HONEYMOON WAS OVER ...

Eric Pooley, 'Exclusive: Rupert Murdoch speaks', *Time*, 28 June 2007.

ON CRITICISMS THAT *THE WALL STREET JOURNAL* READERS' OPINION OF THE PAPER DIMINISHED BECAUSE OF NEWS CORP.'S IMPENDING OWNERSHIP.

Sarah Ellison, *War at* The Wall Street Journal: *Inside the struggle to control an American business empire* (New York: Houghton Mifflin Harcourt Publishing Company, 2010).

ON FOX NEWS BEING FAIR AND BALANCED.

'Interview transcript: Rupert Murdoch and Roger Ailes', *Financial Times* online, 6 October 2006.

ON FOX'S COMPETITION.

A Hearing before the Committee on the Judiciary, House of Representatives, 108th Congress, First Session, 8 May 2003, published in Serial No. 22, Direct Broadcast Satellite Service in the Multichannel Video Distribution Market, US Government Printing Office, Washington DC, 2003.

ON FOX INTERACTIVE MEDIA (FIM).

News Corp. public announcement, 15 July 2005.

ON PRESENTING NEWS AND ENTERTAINMENT.

William Shawcross, *Murdoch: The making of a media empire* (New York: Simon & Schuster, 1997).

ON THE THEN-STRUGGLING LONDON NEWSPAPER, *THE TIMES*, WHICH HE BOUGHT IN 1981.

Michael Leapman, *Arrogant Aussie: The Rupert Murdoch story* (New York: Lyle Stuart, Inc., 1985).

IN RESPONSE TO *THE TIMES* STAFFERS WHO WERE SCEPTICAL OF HIS CLAIMS THAT HE'D GUARANTEE EDITORIAL INDEPENDENCE.

Michael Leapman, *Arrogant Aussie: The Rupert Murdoch story* (New York: Lyle Stuart, Inc., 1985).

TO A *SUNDAY TIMES* EXECUTIVE AT WAPPING.

Neil Chenoweth, *Rupert Murdoch: The untold story of the world's greatest media wizard* (New York: Crown Business, 2011).

ON NEWSPAPERS' ELITISM.

'Interview transcript: Rupert Murdoch and Roger Ailes', *Financial Times* online, 6 October 2006.

ON AMERICAN JOURNALISM.

The Age, November 1983.

ON THE FAILURE OF AMERICAN JOURNALISM TO COMPETE.

Michael Leapman, *Arrogant Aussie: The Rupert Murdoch story* (New York: Lyle Stuart, Inc., 1985).

ON HIS PATENTED BRAND OF TABLOID JOURNALISM,

Greg O'Brien, *Boston* magazine, May 1983.

ON HIS ACQUISITION OF CHICAGO'S *SUN-TIMES*.

Press conference, Chicago, 1 November 1983.

ON WHY READERS SHOULD PASS OVER THE SUNDAY EDITION OF *THE NEW YORK TIMES*.

Wendy Goldman Rohm, *The Murdoch Mission: The digital transformation of a media empire* (New York: John Wiley & Sons, 2002).

A *POST* HEADLINE.

Ken Auletta, 'Promises, Promises', *The New Yorker* online, 2 July 2007.

A *BOSTON HERALD* HEADLINE ON EDWARD KENNEDY.

Ken Auletta, 'Promises, Promises', *The New Yorker* online, 2 July 2007.

ON THE *NEW YORK POST*.

Eric Pooley, 'Exclusive: Rupert Murdoch speaks', *Time,* 28 June 2007.

ON GOOGLE PAYING FOR CONTENT TAKEN FROM THE PRINT MEDIA.

'Rupert Murdoch on the Fate of Newspapers',
www.wallstreetpit.com, 19 November 2009.

ON NEWSPAPERS V. BLOGGERS.

Frances Martel, 'Steve Jobs Fears the Day America "Descends Into a Nation of Bloggers"', www.mediaite.com, 2 June 2010.
Frances Martel, 'Rupert Murdoch Loves the iPad …',
www.mediaite.com, 2 June 2010.

ON CARVING OUT A NICHE IN MEDIA.

'Rupert Murdoch Interview', www.webpublishingblog.com,
15 November 2005.

ON THE BBC.

Clare Matheson, 'Profile: Rupert Murdoch', BBC News
online, 1 August 2007.

ON NEWS CORP. V. STATE-SUPPORTED BROADCASTING.

Bruce Page in collaboration with Elaine Potter, *The Murdoch Archipelago* (London: Simon & Schuster UK, 2003).

ON HIS ACQUISITION OF *THE SUN*.

William Shawcross, *Murdoch: The making of a media empire* (New York: Simon & Schuster, 1997).

ON THE POPULAR 'PAGE THREE GIRLS' IN *THE SUN*.

Wendy Goldman Rohm, *The Murdoch Mission: The digital transformation of a media empire* (New York: John Wiley & Sons, 2002).

ON A NEWSPAPER'S POSITION, TO HAROLD EVANS, *THE SUNDAY TIMES* EDITOR.

William Shawcross, *Murdoch: The making of a media empire* (New York: Simon & Schuster, 1997).

ON ACCUSATIONS THAT NDS (NEWS CORP'S PAY-TV SMARTCARD SECURITY UNIT) IS PROMOTING PIRACY ATTACKS ON THE COMPETITION.

Rupert Murdoch, Twitter, 29 March 2012.

ON NEWS CORP.'S BROADBAND PENETRATION.

A Hearing before the Committee on the Judiciary, House of Representatives, 108th Congress, First Session, 8 May 2003, published in Serial No. 22, Direct Broadcast Satellite Service in the Multichannel Video Distribution Market, US Government Printing Office, Washington DC, 2003.

ON CNN'S FAULTS.

William Shawcross, *Murdoch: The making of a media empire* (New York: Simon & Schuster, 1997).

ON BOOK PUBLISHING.

Steve Stecklow and Martin Peers, 'Murdoch's Role as Proprietor, Journalist and Plans for Dow Jones', *The Wall Street Journal* online, 6 June 2007.

ON RISKING THE JOBS OF 200 EMPLOYEES WHO WORKED AT *NEWS OF THE WORLD*.

'Uncorrected Transcript of Oral Evidence to be published as HC 903-ii: House of Commons/oral evidence taken before the culture, media and sport select committee/Phone Hacking/Tuesday 19 July 2011/Rupert Murdoch and James Murdoch/Rebekah Brooks', London, House of Commons Information Office, prepared 25 July 2011, published online at www.parliament.uk.

ON CRITICS AND ENEMIES.

Eric Pooley, 'Exclusive: Rupert Murdoch speaks', *Time*, 28 June 2007.

ON SUCCESS AND SCAR TISSUE.

Clare Matheson, 'Profile: Rupert Murdoch', BBC News online, 1 August 2007.

ON THE PRINTERS' UNION STRIKE AFTER MURDOCH MOVED THE LONDON *TIMES* TO WAPPING.

Uncommon Knowledge, hosted by Peter M Robinson, recorded 5 February 2010, posted online 22 July 2011.

ON THE ECONOMY.

Eric Savitz, 'D: News Corp.'s Murdoch "mystified" by YHOO's failure to do MSFT deal; sees recession; will he vote for Obama?', *Barron's* online, 28 May 2008.

WHEN ASKED, 'OF ALL THE THINGS IN YOUR BUSINESS EMPIRE, WHAT GIVES YOU THE MOST PLEASURE?'

Ken Auletta, 'Promises, Promises', *The New Yorker* online, 2 July 2007.

ON HIS PRESENCE IN THE NEWSROOM.

Ken Auletta, 'Promises, Promises', *The New Yorker* online, 2 July 2007.

ON ACCOUNTABILITY.

Steve Stecklow and Martin Peers, 'Murdoch's Role as Proprietor, Journalist and Plans for Dow Jones', *The Wall Street Journal* online, 6 June 2007.

ON ACCUSATIONS OF *NEWS OF THE WORLD* BREAKING THE LAW TO GET NEWS SCOOPS.

'Uncorrected Transcript of Oral Evidence to be published as HC 903-ii: House of Commons/oral evidence taken before the culture, media and sport select committee/Phone Hacking/Tuesday 19 July 2011/Rupert Murdoch and James Murdoch/Rebekah Brooks', London, House of Commons Information Office, prepared 25 July 2011, published online at www.parliament.uk.

AN EMPLOYEE'S RESPONSE.

'Sun Valley: Conference "very bearish," Murdoch says', *The Wall Street Journal* online, 9 July 2009.

ON FIGHTING BACK AS A DETERRENCE.

Michael Leapman, *Arrogant Aussie: The Rupert Murdoch story* (New York: Lyle Stuart, Inc., 1985).

ON *POST* WRITERS' ASSERTION THAT 'IT'S OUR NEWSPAPER, TOO' IN A PETITION.

Michael Leapman, *Arrogant Aussie: The Rupert Murdoch story* (New York: Lyle Stuart, Inc., 1985).

ON HIS DECISION TO FIRE 148 *POST* STAFFERS WHO HAD SIGNED THE PETITION.

Michael Leapman, *Arrogant Aussie: The Rupert Murdoch story* (New York: Lyle Stuart, Inc., 1985).

ON EMPLOYEES UNHAPPY WORKING FOR HIM.

Richard Hack, *Clash of the Titans* (Beverly Hills, Ca.: New Millennium Press, 2003).

ON AMERICAN UNIONS.

'Some Unions Assailed', *The New York Times*, 21 April 1978.

ON CONFLICT OF INTEREST.

Michael Leapman, *Arrogant Aussie: The Rupert Murdoch story* (New York: Lyle Stuart, Inc., 1985).

ON MONOPOLIES.

Wendy Goldman Rohm, *The Murdoch Mission: The digital transformation of a media empire* (New York: John Wiley & Sons, 2002).
Richard Hack, *Clash of the Titans* (Beverly Hills, Ca.: New Millennium Press, 2003).

On conscience and newspapers' societal role.

Wendy Goldman Rohm, *The Murdoch Mission: The digital transformation of a media empire* (New York: John Wiley & Sons, 2002).

On the citizen's right to know.

Bruce Page in collaboration with Elaine Potter, *The Murdoch Archipelago* (London: Simon & Schuster UK, 2003).

On conscience and consistency in a newspaper's editorial views.

Bruce Page in collaboration with Elaine Potter, *The Murdoch Archipelago* (London: Simon & Schuster UK, 2003).

On his deep-rooted ties to Australia.

Bruce Page in collaboration with Elaine Potter, *The Murdoch Archipelago* (London: Simon & Schuster UK, 2003).

On striking while the iron is hot.

Richard Hack, *Clash of the Titans* (Beverly Hills, Ca.: New Millennium Press, 2003).

On himself.

William Shawcross, 'Murdoch's New Life', *Vanity Fair*, October 1999.

Murdoch's motto.

Richard Hack, *Clash of the Titans* (Beverly Hills, Ca.: New Millennium Press, 2003).

On News Corp.'s critics.

Speech for News Corp. employees worldwide, broadcast from New York City, 9 May 2007.

ON RUNNING A STORY ABOUT THE CALL GIRL WHO BROUGHT DOWN JOHN PROFUMO, THE THEN-SECRETARY OF STATE FOR WAR.

William Shawcross, *Murdoch: The making of a media empire* (New York: Simon & Schuster, 1997).

ON NEWSPAPER SNOBS.

Sue Vander Hook, *Rupert Murdoch: News Corporation magnate* (Edina, Minn.: ABDO Publishing Company, 2011).

ON TRADITION.

Media Summit, sponsored by The McGraw-Hill Companies, New York City, 8 February 2007. Interviewed by *Bloomberg Businessweek* editor Steve Adler.

ON GREAT JOURNALISM.

'The Dawn of a New Age of Discovery: Media 2006', lecture at the Annual Livery Lecture, the Worshipful Company of Stationers and Newspaper Makers, London, 13 March 2006.

ON THE DOGGED PERSISTENCE AND PROFESSIONALISM OF HIS EMPLOYEES.

'Rupert Murdoch's Inaugural Margaret Thatcher Lecture', *The Guardian*, 21 October 2010.

ON THE POTENTIAL OF PRINT.

Annual shareholders' address, Asia Society Museum, New York City, 20 October 2006.

ON MAINTAINING THE LEAD DOG POSITION.

Bear Stearns Media Conference, Palm Beach, Florida, 1 March 2008.

ON MASS APPEAL.

William Shawcross, *Murdoch: The making of a media empire* (New York: Simon & Schuster, 1997).

On the old and new broadcasting paradigms.

'Speech by Rupert Murdoch to the American Society of Newspaper Editors', News Corp. press release, Washington DC, 13 April 2005.

On the liberating powers of communication technology.

Speech for News Corp. advertisers, London, 1 September 1993.

On media flourishing in China.

Speech for think tank the Party School of the China Communist Party Central Committee, Beijing, 9 October 2003.

On defending ideas in a free society.

'Rupert Murdoch's Inaugural Margaret Thatcher Lecture', *The Guardian*, 21 October 2010.

On RM's use of media to peddle political influence.

A Hearing before the Committee on the Judiciary, House of Representatives, 108th Congress, First Session, 8 May 2003, published in Serial No. 22, Direct Broadcast Satellite Service in the Multichannel Video Distribution Market, US Government Printing Office, Washington DC, 2003.

On bloggers.

'Rupert Murdoch's Inaugural Margaret Thatcher Lecture', *The Guardian*, 21 October 2010.

On virtuous publishing and a vigorous press.

'Rupert Murdoch's Inaugural Margaret Thatcher Lecture', *The Guardian*, 21 October 2010.

On responsibility.

Widely attributed to RM online.

ON OWNERSHIP AFFECTING THE EDITORIAL PRODUCT.

Clare Matheson, 'Profile: Rupert Murdoch', BBC News online, 1 August 2007.

ON HAVING A STERLING REPUTATION.

James Boyd-Wallis, 'Paying the Price for a Poor Reputation', Director of Finance Online, 5 July 2010.

ON BEING ASKED WHO WAS RESPONSIBLE FOR THE PHONE TAPPING.

'Uncorrected Transcript of Oral Evidence to be published as HC 903-ii: House of Commons/oral evidence taken before the culture, media and sport select committee/Phone Hacking/Tuesday 19 July 2011/Rupert Murdoch and James Murdoch/Rebekah Brooks', London, House of Commons Information Office, prepared 25 July 2011, published online at www.parliament.uk.

ON INDEPENDENT DECISION-MAKING.

'Control Freakonomics', *CNBC Business* magazine, March 2012.

ON EDUCATION.

'Murdoch Interview with Alan Jones', *The Sydney Morning Herald*, 7 April 2004.

ON BEING AN OUTSIDER OF THE FIRMLY ENTRENCHED BRITISH SYSTEM.

Alexander Cockburn, *The Village Voice*, 1976.

ON FORMER CBS NEWS ANCHOR DAN RATHER'S NOTION THAT THE GOVERNMENT SHOULD BAIL OUT NEWSPAPERS.

Uncommon Knowledge, hosted by Peter M Robinson, recorded 5 February 2010, posted online 22 July 2011.

ON GOOGLE PASSING UP MYSPACE.

Spencer Reiss, 'His Space', *Wired*, July 2006.

On the urgency in buying MySpace.

Eric Savitz, 'D: News Corp.'s Murdoch "mystified" by YHOO's failure to do MSFT deal; sees recession; will he vote for Obama?', *Barron's* online, 28 May 2008.

On MySpace's potential.

'Rupert Murdoch Has Potential', *Esquire* online, 11 September 2008.

On MySpace's valuation.

Speech for the Goldman Sachs Communacopia XVI Conference, New York City, 18 September 2007.

On risky dot-com acquisitions.

News Corp. General Meeting, Adelaide, Australia, October 2000.

On MySpace changing with its new corporate ownership.

Clare Matheson, 'Profile: Rupert Murdoch', BBC News online, 1 August 2007.

On writing off MySpace's US$545 million net loss.

Rupert Murdoch, Twitter, 29 June 2011.

On acquiring Internet properties.

'Remarks by the Chairman, Annual Meeting of Stockholders', News Corp. press release, 21 October 2005.

On Steve Jobs's iPad.

Press conference, New York City, 2 February 2011.

On context and content.

Uncommon Knowledge, hosted by Peter M Robinson, recorded 5 February 2010, posted online 22 July 2011.

ON PAYING FOR CONTENT.

Erick Schonfeld, 'Murdoch Warns That without eTablets, "Newspapers Will Go Out of Business"', www.techcrunch.com, 17 November 2009.

ON THE FUTURE OF NEWSPAPERS.

Spencer Reiss, 'His Space', *Wired*, July 2006.

ON TABLETS' DIGITAL INK AND ECOLOGY.

'Rupert Murdoch's Digital Newspaper "The Daily" Debuts Today', www.ibtimes.com, 2 February 2011.

ON NOT BUYING AOL AFTER MICROSOFT CO-FOUNDER BILL GATES DISSUADED HIM.

Richard Hack, *Clash of the Titans* (Beverly Hills, Ca.: New Millennium Press, 2003).

ON INVESTING IN THE INTERNET.

Conference call with Wall Street analysts, 10 August 2005.

ON MONETISING SEARCH ENGINES AND NEWS AGGREGATORS.

Dan Freed, 'Murdoch Talks Media', www.thestreet.com, 2 July 2009.

ON NEWS CORP.'S GOAL.

Steve Stecklow and Martin Peers, 'Murdoch's Role as Proprietor, Journalist and Plans for Dow Jones', *The Wall Street Journal* online, 6 June 2007.

ON GOOGLE.

Steve Stecklow and Martin Peers, 'Murdoch's Role as Proprietor, Journalist and Plans for Dow Jones', *The Wall Street Journal* online, 6 June 2007.

ON THE POTENTIAL OF THE DIGITAL MEDIUM.

Speech for the World Media Summit, Beijing, China,
9 October 2009.

ON TRADITIONAL PRINT'S ELECTRONIC EVOLUTION.

'Rupert and *The News*', www.bytesdaily.blogspot.com,
11 July 2011.

ON THE WEB EMPOWERING PEOPLE.

Spencer Reiss, 'His Space', *Wired*, July 2006.

ON CENSORING THE INTERNET.

Johnnie L Roberts, 'Murdoch's New Groove',
www.thedailybeast.com, 12 February 2006.

ON THE OFT-QUOTED MANTRA BY ONLINE PIRATES THAT 'INFORMATION WANTS TO BE FREE.'

Speech for the World Media Summit, Beijing, China,
9 October 2009.
Uncommon Knowledge, hosted by Peter M Robinson, recorded
5 February 2010, posted online 22 July 2011.

ON CONTENT BEING KING.

Uncommon Knowledge, hosted by Peter M Robinson, recorded
5 February 2010, posted online 22 July 2011.

ON THE PROLIFERATION OF BROADBAND.

Johnnie L Roberts, 'Murdoch's New Groove',
www.thedailybeast.com, 12 February 2006.

ON THE GENERATIONAL DIVIDE ON COMPUTERS.

'Speech by Rupert Murdoch to the American Society of
Newspaper Editors', News Corp. press release, Washington
DC, 13 April 2005.

ON THE SPEED OF INFORMATION IN OUR DIGITAL AGE.

'The Asian Renaissance: Economic and political challenges of the 21st century', address by Rupert Murdoch at the Yomiuiri International Economic Society, Tokyo, 6 November 2006.

ON THE IRAQ WAR.

Jason Deans, 'Murdoch: US must ditch "inferiority complex"', *The Guardian*, 3 April 2003.

ON CHARGES THAT NEWS CORP. SHAPED THE IRAQ WAR'S AGENDA.

'Who Will Shape the Agenda?', World Economic Forum, 26 January 2007.

ON THE US HOUSING BUBBLE.

Tyler Durden (pseudonym), 'Rupert Murdoch Interview: "Economy weak; danger of inflation great"', www.seekingalpha.com, 28 April 2009.

ON *THE NEW YORK TIMES* FAVOURING PRESIDENT OBAMA.

'Murdoch: MSNBC, CNN "tend to be Democrats," *New York Times* carries Obama's water', www.huffingtonpost.com, 6 June 2010.

ON GOVERNMENT REGULATION AND THE FREE MARKET.

Tyler Durden (pseudonym), 'Rupert Murdoch Interview: "Economy weak; danger of inflation great"', www.seekingalpha.com, 28 April 2009.

ON RECESSION AND THE OBAMA ADMINISTRATION.

'Rupert Murdoch on the Fate of Newspapers', www.wallstreetpit.com, 19 November 2009.

ON POLITICAL YIN AND YANG IN CHINA.

Wendy Goldman Rohm, *The Murdoch Mission: The digital transformation of a media empire* (New York: John Wiley & Sons, 2002).

ON CHINA CURIOUSLY BEREFT OF COMMUNISM.

William Shawcross, 'Murdoch's New Life', *Vanity Fair*, October 1999.

ON CHINA'S 'OPEN DOOR'.

'The Asian Renaissance: Economic and political challenges of the 21st century', address by Rupert Murdoch at the Yomiuiri International Economic Society, Tokyo, 6 November 2006.

ON CHINESE REPRESSION OF THE NEWS.

'The Asian Renaissance: Economic and political challenges of the 21st century', address by Rupert Murdoch at the Yomiuiri International Economic Society, Tokyo, 6 November 2006.

ON THE CONTRAST BETWEEN CHINA AND INDIA IN THE FLOW OF INFORMATION.

'The Asian Renaissance: Economic and political challenges of the 21st century', address by Rupert Murdoch at the Yomiuiri International Economic Society, Tokyo, 6 November 2006.

ON THE BYZANTINE CHINESE MARKET.

News Corp. media analysts' briefing, reported by Indiantelevision.com, 8 February 2007.

ON PATIENCE WITH CHINA.

Media event, New York City, 8 February 2007.

ON CHINA LOWERING THE BAMBOO CURTAIN.

Media conference, New York City, 16 September 2005.

ON ESTABLISHING A MEDIA FOOTHOLD IN CHINA.

Meeting with Ding Guangen, leading member of the Political

Bureau and Secretariat of the Chinese Communist Party
Central Committee, Great Hall of the People, Tiananmen
Square, Beijing, 24 October 1997.

On China embracing new technologies.

Keynote address, International Federation of the Periodical
Press World Publishers' Conference, Tokyo, 15 May 1997.

The Iraq War

Roy Greenslade, 'Their Master's Voice', *The Guardian*,
16 February 2003.

On optimism, oil, and the Iraq War.

Julia Day, 'Murdoch Praises Blair's "Courage"', *The Guardian*,
11 February 2003.

On PM Tony Blair's support of President George Bush's Iraq War.

Roy Greenslade, 'Their Master's Voice', *The Guardian*,
16 February 2003.

On his reputed power on Capitol Hill.

Richard Hack, *Clash of the Titans* (Beverly Hills, Ca.: New
Millennium Press, 2003).

On coverage of Watergate and Richard Nixon, whom he supported.

William Shawcross, *Murdoch: The making of a media empire*
(New York: Simon & Schuster, 1997).

On the cost of bucking the establishment.

Richard Hack, *Clash of the Titans* (Beverly Hills, Ca.: New
Millennium Press, 2003).

ON MURDERED 13-YEAR-OLD MILLY DOWLER, WHOSE PHONE WAS HACKED, GIVING HER PARENTS FALSE HOPE THAT SHE WAS STILL ALIVE.

'"Shocked, Appalled, and Ashamed"...', *The Sydney Morning Herald*, 20 July 2011.
Douglas Stanglin, 'A "Shaken" Rupert Murdoch Meets with the Family of Murdered Girl', *USA Today* online, 15 July 2011.

ON THE PHONE-HACKING SCANDAL.

Stephen Mayne, '2010 News Corp AGM Transcript', The Mayne Report, 15 October 2010.

ON HOW NEWS CORP. HANDLED THE PHONE-HACKING SCANDAL.

Andrew Edgecliffe-Johnson and Kara Scannel, 'Murdoch Admits to "minor mistakes"', *Financial Times*, 14 July 2011.

THE WALL STREET JOURNAL'S VIGOROUS DEFENCE OF ITS BOSS.

'Review & Outlook: News and its critics', *The Wall Street Journal*, 18 July 2011.

ON *NEWS OF THE WORLD* PERMANENTLY SUSPENDING PUBLICATION.

'*News of the World* to Close amid Hacking Scandal', BBC News online, 7 July 2011.

BACKING REBEKAH BROOKS, *NEWS OF THE WORLD* EDITOR.

Kate Holton and Jodie Ginsberg, 'Murdoch Defends Paper as Cameron Pledges Hacking Problem', Reuters Edition US, 6 July 2011.

ON *NEWS OF THE WORLD* EDITOR REBEKAH BROOKS'S ADMISSION OF WRONGDOING GIVEN AT A PARLIAMENTARY HEARING.

'Uncorrected Transcript of Oral Evidence to be published as HC 903-ii: House of Commons/oral evidence taken before

the culture, media and sport select committee/Phone
Hacking/Tuesday 19 July 2011/Rupert Murdoch and James
Murdoch/Rebekah Brooks', London, House of Commons
Information Office, prepared 25 July 2011, published online
at www.parliament.uk.

ON ALL THE CRITICISM.

Bruce Orwall, 'In Interview, Murdoch Defends News Corp.',
The Wall Street Journal, 14 July 2011.

ON CREDIBILITY WITH HIS NEWSPAPER'S READERSHIP.

'Uncorrected Transcript of Oral Evidence to be published as
HC 903-ii: House of Commons/oral evidence taken before
the culture, media and sport select committee/Phone
Hacking/Tuesday 19 July 2011/Rupert Murdoch and James
Murdoch/Rebekah Brooks', London, House of Commons
Information Office, prepared 25 July 2011, published online
at www.parliament.uk.

**ON POTENTIAL FALLOUT TO THE COMPANY BECAUSE OF THE
PHONE-HACKING SCANDAL.**

Bruce Orwall, 'In Interview, Murdoch Defends News Corp.',
The Wall Street Journal, 14 July 2011.

ON THE LAUNCH OF *THE SUN*.

A note to the staff of News Corp., 17 February 2012.

**ON ACCOUNTABILITY OF NEWS CORP. IN THE WAKE OF ITS
SYSTEMIC PHONE-TAPPING SCANDAL.**

'A Letter from Rupert Murdoch: Issues surrounding *News of
the World*', News Corp. Annual Report, 2011.

NEWS CORP.'S APOLOGY FOR HACKING CELEBRITIES' PHONES.

News International statement, 11 April 2011.

On betrayal, to the British Parliament on the phone hacking scandal.

Mark Memmott, 'Murdoch: "This is the most humble day of my life"', NPR, 19 July 2011.

Closing statement to the Culture, Media and Sport Select Committee.

'Uncorrected Transcript of Oral Evidence to be published as HC 903-ii: House of Commons/oral evidence taken before the culture, media and sport select committee/Phone Hacking/Tuesday 19 July 2011/Rupert Murdoch and James Murdoch/Rebekah Brooks', London, House of Commons Information Office, prepared 25 July 2011, published online at www.parliament.uk.

George Beahm, the editor of the internationally best-selling *I, Steve: Steve Jobs in his own words*, is a former Army major who served on active duty, in the National Guard, and the Army Reserves. He has published dozens of nonfiction books.

Beahm lives in Hampton Roads, Virginia.